English for me

Eric Boagey

Head of English, Eastfields High School, Merton

University Tutorial Press

Published by University Tutorial Press Ltd
842 Yeovil Road, Slough SL1 4JQ

ISBN 0 7231 0777 7

Published 1979

© E. J. Boagey 1979

Printed by Eyre & Spottiswoode Limited at Grosvenor Press Portsmouth

Acknowledgements

The author is indebted to the following for permission to use copyright material.

Ronald Blythe for the extract from *Akenfield* (Penguin Books Ltd.);
Adrian Henri for 'Autobiography' from *Penguin Modern Poets 10* (Penguin Books Ltd.);
John Fuller for 'Alex at the Barber's' from *Fairground Music* (Chatto and Windus Ltd.);
Macdonald and Jane's Publishers Ltd. for the extract from *Our Kate* by Catherine Cookson;
Ken Smith for 'Family Group' from *The Pity* (Jonathan Cape Ltd.);
Victor Gollancz Ltd. for the extract from *I Chose to Climb* by Christian Bonington;
George Tardios for 'Sea-Signs' from *New Poems 1976–77* PEN Anthology;
Constable Publishers for the extracts from *This Time Next Week* by Leslie Thomas;
Jonathan Cape Ltd. for 'Letter to Barbados' by Ted Walker from *Gloves to the Hangman*;
Janet Hitchman for the extract from *The King of the Barbareens* by Janet Hitchman (Penguin Books Ltd.);
J. M. Dent & Sons Ltd. for 'Warning' by Jenny Joseph from *Rose in the Afternoon and Other Poems*;
Jonathan Cape Ltd. and Mrs. Ellen Wright for the extract from *Black Boy* by Richard Wright;
Stanley Cook for his poems 'For Them' from *New Poetry 1* and 'Schoolday' from *Signs of Life*;
Jonathan Cape Ltd. and the Estate of Hermann Hesse for the extract from 'Childhood of the Magician' by Hermann Hesse from *Autobiographical Writings*, ed. Theodore Ziolkowski, translated by Denver Lindley;
Frank Ormsby for 'My Friend Havelock Ellis' from *A Store of Candles* (Oxford University Press);
Mrs. Sonia Brownwell Orwell and Martin Secker and Warburg

Ltd. for the extract from *Down and Out in Paris and London* by George Orwell;

Extracts from *The House of Elrig* by Gavin Maxwell (Longmans, Green, 1965, pp. 148–152; Penguin Books, 1974, pp. 165–170). Copyright © 1965 by Gavin Maxwell reprinted by permission of Penguin Books Ltd.;

Wes Magee for 'All Night Disco' from *New Poems 1975* PEN Anthology;

BBC Publications for the extract from *A Child in the Forest* by Winifred Foley;

Eddie Wainwright for 'Honda 175' from *New Poetry 1;*

George Allen & Unwin (Publishers) Ltd. for the extract 'How to Grow Old' from *Portraits from Memory* by Bertrand Russell;

Graham Allen for 'Poem for my Father' from *Out of the Dark* (Christopher Davies, Publishers).

Contents

An Akenfield Boy	Ronald Blythe	1
Autobiography	Adrian Henri	9
A Confession	Jack London	13
Alex at the Barber's	John Fuller	23
Childhood Agonies	Catherine Cookson	25
Family Group	Ken Smith	35
First Climb	Christian Bonington	38
Sea-Signs	George Tardios	48
Doing a Bunk	Leslie Thomas	51
Letter to Barbados	Ted Walker	63
The Last Chance	Janet Hitchman	66
Warning	Jenny Joseph	75
Seeing an Angel	Richard Wright	77
For Them	Stanley Cook	87
The Little Man	Hermann Hesse	90
My Friend Havelock Ellis	Frank Ormsby	98
Seventeen Hours a Day	George Orwell	100
Schoolday	Stanley Cook	109
Dinner at the Castle	Gavin Maxwell	113
All Night Disco	Wes Magee	122
At Sixteen	Winifred Foley	124
Honda 175	Eddie Wainwright	136
How to Grow Old	Bertrand Russell	139
Poem for my Father	Graham Allen	145

Preface

English is one of the few subjects in which pupils have an opportunity of expressing something about their own experience of life and my aim in making this selection of prose and poetry has been to provide this opportunity over as wide a field as possible. The stress throughout is on authenticity and sincerity – the writer describing his own reaction to events he has lived through and understood. There is, therefore, nothing that is fictitious or purely intellectual; there is simply the truth of personal experience. Thus, for instance, Catherine Cookson expresses the feeling of humiliation at being made to go to the pawnshop as a child; Richard Wright describes his struggle to remain true to his agnosticism in the face of attempts to convert him to belief; Gavin Maxwell portrays the agonies of adolescence in an indifferent adult society; Winifred Foley shows how she suffered from the pride of a young girl in love; Herman Hesse recalls the powerful urge towards independence and self-assertion that exists in the child before he has accepted the need to conform; and Christian Bonington narrates the events in his boyhood that revealed his passion for climbing. Quite by chance, the main theme of the selection emerges as the suffering and the struggles that are necessary before the young person can come to terms with the adult world. This is worth pondering on, since it is intended that the experiences depicted in the narratives and poems should find an echo in the lives of the pupils themselves – not in the external events, such as visiting a pawnshop, climbing mountains or going to hunt balls, but in the feelings that accompany these and similar events – the pride, the embarrassments, the persistence, the rebelliousness, the remorse, the sense of injustice and a sheer zest for living.

The work that arises from the material in the book is intended to develop oral and written expression in the fourth and fifth years of the secondary school. After the prose passages – all of them written in the first person – pupils are asked to conduct an interview with the author, only they themselves represent the author and they answer the questions as though they were being interviewed on radio or television. The questions are concerned more with interpretation and motivation than with fact and the answers cannot be quoted from the text: they must be expressed in the pupil's own words, based on the content of the passage and what can be reasonably inferred from it. Thought and understanding are needed, but an answer is never 'wrong' providing it can be sensibly justified.

The interview is followed by a class conversation which leads from the topics of the passage into an exchange of personal experience. The class sits in an informal group, preferably not at desks, and the teacher leads off with one of the questions. The ensuing conversation will tend to take an unpredictable course, as most conversations do, depending for its direction on the associations sparked off in the minds of those listening. When the talk dries up on one topic, the teacher introduces something new; and he copes with the occasional silence by talking about his own experience, for in this situation he is both guiding the talk and participating in it on the same level as his pupils. It leads to an interesting change in the relationship between teacher and pupil.

The language work is aimed at developing a strong vocabulary and includes the study of jargon, foreign words, poetic expression and dialect. There are occasional excursions into tape-recording, drama, role-play and improvisation, but the main creative emphasis is on personal writing in the form of essays of ideas and comment, short stories, descriptive narratives and the expression of individual experience. The subjects have some links with the prose passages and some of them will have been touched upon in the conversation lessons by way of preparation.

The poetry, like the prose, has been chosen because it is a personal statement or an expression of experience that might find a response in the lives of the pupils themselves. The work based upon it is, first, to study the poet's language, perhaps to solve one or two of the textual difficulties, and secondly, to write either prose or poetry on a related theme. The form of the poem is usually free verse and therefore provides a simple model for poetic composition. It is not difficult to get pupils to write poetry, providing that the subjects suggested are within their range and that they are assured that technique is of secondary importance.

The English Language examination in the fifth form demands proficiency in comprehension, oracy and written composition. I have tried to develop this proficiency by basing the work on literature that is personal in tone and which might, therefore, illuminate one or two areas of the pupils' own experiences. In this way the preparation for an examination need not be wholly divorced from a preparation for expressing and understanding oneself.

E.J.B.

An Akenfield Boy
Ronald Blythe

Akenfield is a portrait of a village in Suffolk as seen through
the eyes of the people who live and work there. Leonard
Thompson, a farm worker, talks about his childhood at the
beginning of the century.

I walked two miles to school. There were so many children you could
hardly squeeze in the room. All the same, it was very cold in the
winter. Most of the boys had suits and boots on with nothing underneath. Every now and then we used to have to stand on the outside
of our desks and mark-time to get our circulation back. We did
left-right, left-right for about five minutes – good God, what a row
we made! Later on, I heard this sound again in Gallipoli. It seemed
homely and familiar. We must have been bashing some landing-
stage. The school was useless. The farmers came and took boys away
from it when they felt like it, the parson raided it for servants. The
teacher was a respectable woman who did her best. Sometimes she
would bring the *Daily Graphic* down and show us the news. I looked
forward to leaving school so that I could get educated. I knew that
education was in books, not in school: there were no books there. I
was a child when I left but I already knew that our 'learning' was
rubbish, that our food was rubbish and that I should end as rubbish
if I didn't look out.

When I was six we moved to another house. It was a tied-cottage
with a thatched roof and handsome beams. My father said, 'We shall
be better off, boys, we shall have a nice spring of water just across
the road, and that will be a great relief. Also we shall have a nice big

garden with two apple trees, a Doctor Harvey and a Blenheim Orange.' We moved to this house in 1904. As soon as we got there, mother went stone-picking in the fields. She didn't have to do this because we were living in a tied-cottage but because we had to buy some new clothes. We helped her when we got back from school at five o'clock. She had to pick up twenty-four bushels of stones a day to get 2s. Each parish had to mend its own lanes then and the stones were used for this. A tumbril was put in the field and a line was chalked round it. When you had filled it up to the line you got the 2s. It would take the whole day. We did it every minute we weren't at school and all through the holidays. It was all I can remember.

But during the harvest holiday we had a change – gleaning. The women would meet and say, 'Is Scarlets ready for gleaning yet? Is Great Mosses?' – these were the names of the fields. They meant, not has the field been cut but have they cleared the 'policeman'. The policeman was the name given to the last trave or stook which the farmers would leave standing in the middle of the field so they could have time to rake-up all the loose corn they could before the gleaners arrived. There was one farmer who made a habit of keeping the gleaners waiting and one night a young man stole the 'policeman'. The next morning the gleaners hurried in and gleaned masses – the field hadn't been raked, you see. The whole village was laughing – except the farmer. He raked-up quick the next year, I can tell you. I gleaned all my boyhood. I ran away from it once but came to grief, and since the results have been with me all my life, I will tell you about it. When I was six I got fed up with being in the gleaning-field with all the women, so I ran off to help the boy who worked the cattle-cake machine. In no time my hand was caught and my fingers were squashed. The farmer was just coming up by the granary on his horse when he heard me screaming. 'What have you been up to, you young scamp?' he shouted. 'My fingers – they're in the cake-breaker!' And he said – I shall never forget it – 'Get you off home then!' But when he saw my hand he changed his tune and said, 'Get up to the house.' The farmer's wife tied some rag round my hand and took me home and my mother wheeled me miles to the doctor's in a pram. My sister was home from service, so she came with us and held me while the doctor scraped grease out of my wounds with a knife, stitched up one finger, cut another, pared it like a stick and tied what was left to the bone, and then moved on to the next finger. I lifted the roof, I can tell you. There was no anaesthetic, nothing.

My sister began to faint and the doctor got on to her something terrific. 'Damn silly girl – clear off outside if you can't stand it! Fetch my groom in.' So the groom came and held me until it was finished. All the time the doctor worked he shouted. 'What did you do it for? Why? Damn little nuisance! Stupid little fool!'

Nobody used pity then, and especially not to children, and particularly not to boys. The farmer told my father and he said, 'I'll give him something to think about when I get home!' It was harvest so it was late when he returned home. 'Where's that boy Leonard?' he said. 'I'm going to give him a good hiding.' 'He's gone to bed, he's had enough,' said mother. My father didn't realize how bad it was, you see. The tops of three of my fingers had been cut off. So he didn't touch me.

There were a lot of hidings then. My father was a good man and didn't like giving them to us, but some people did. Father never smoked or drank, and he looked after his children. He had a wonderful character in the parish. He would go to work with three-quarters of a loaf of bread and a little bit of cheese, and maybe a couple of onions, but when we ran to meet him after his day's work, he would give us the cheese. He had saved it for us. 'I can do without that,' he would say. We were thrashed a lot at school. Fathers would be ordered to the school to hold their sons while the mistress thrashed them. Most of the teachers were big thrashers. But we were tough, very tough. Everybody said, don't-don't, to boys then and after a while we didn't listen. We were wondering how we could get away.

I left school when I was thirteen, on April 20th when the corn was low. I helped my mother pulling up docks in the Big Field for a shilling an acre, which my mother took. She could see that I was too big to have money taken from me like this, so when the farmer came round she said, 'Can't you give my boy a proper job?' She meant a regular job with a wage. But the farmer just laughed and rode away. So the next week I tried my luck at another farm. Mr. Wakeling, this farmer, was very tall and he had three sons of about eighteen to twenty-one who were all over six feet. They all stood looking down at me and smiling. 'So you are thirteen and you have left school, but what can you do?' 'I can do anything.' 'Well, there's a mangold field over there – you do that.'

'What are you going to get?' asked my mother when I told her. 'I never asked and he never said,' I replied. It was the beginning of being grown-up.

I had a week in this field, singling mangolds, and I did well because I had often done the job before, after school. The farmer came and looked and said, 'You've done well, my little man. How much have I got to give you?' 'My mother said half-a-crown but perhaps you would sooner give me a rise.' But the farmer thought half-a-crown was good, which was what I got for sixty hours' work. When the harvest came along, the boy who was doing the milking, and who was seventeen and strong, was told to load corn and I had to take over the cows. The farmer's riding ponies and then his sons' ponies were added. Then the farmer said, 'You'll have to work Sundays now, but I shall be giving you another sixpence.' So I got 3s. a week. Mother said, 'How lucky you are!' Shortly after this my father came to grief with his farmer and we had to leave the tied-cottage. We moved down by the river and when we were settled father took my brother and myself to his new employer and, twizzling me round so that I could be seen, said, 'Here's a good strong boy. I want 4s. 6d. a week for him.' 'We'll see about that at the end of the week,' said the farmer. Then my father made my brother stand forward – he was fifteen – and said, 'Look what a fine lad. I want 8s. a week for him.' The farmer thought a minute, looked us up and down and said, 'All right.'

The second week that I was at this new farm I had to drive a herd of cattle to Ipswich. I was thirteen and had lived only ten miles away all my life, but I had never been to this big town before. The farmer went ahead in his trap and waited for me at Ipswich market. He sold the cows and bought some more, and told me to drive them back to the farm. Most of my work was like this, walking cattle along the roads backwards and forwards to the market – about twenty-five miles a day. The farmer was a dealer. I stayed with him a year and four months and was paid 4s. 6d. a week. And then I got into a hell of a row. I'd driven a flock of sheep from Ipswich and the next morning they found that one had died. The farmer was in a terrible stew. He ran down the field and met my mother on her way to chapel and told her all about it. I had driven the sheep too hard, he said. 'And you drive boys too hard!' said my mother – she had no fear at all. Well, the truth of the matter is that she said a lot of things she'd only thought until then, and so I left the farm. It must seem that there was a war between farmers and their men in those days. I think there was, particularly in Suffolk. These employers were famous for their meanness. They took all they could from the men and boys who worked their land. They bought their life's strength for as little as they could. They wore us out without a thought because, with the big families, there was a continuous supply of labour. Fourteen young men left the village in 1909–11 to join the army. There wasn't a recruiting drive, they just escaped. And some people just changed their sky, as they say, and I was one of them.

(from *Akenfield*)

The Interview

Imagine that you are Leonard Thompson and that you are being interviewed about the part of your life you have just described. Using the evidence of the passage, what would you say in answer to the following questions?

1. What do you mean when you say you would *end as rubbish* if you didn't look out?
2. You say you were picking up stones all through the holidays – and presumably you didn't enjoy it very much! What would you rather have been doing?
3. As you say *nobody used pity then* – but do you think the lack of pity made you tougher and more able to stand up to the difficulties of later life?
4. You speak very well of your parents. What did you particularly admire about your father?
5. On which occasions would you say you benefited from your mother's character?
6. You didn't know what wage you would be paid for your first job. You replied to your mother's question: *I never asked and he never said.* Why didn't you ask? It would seem the obvious thing to do.
7. What were the main reasons for your wanting to leave Akenfield, or to *change your sky*, as you say?
8. Now you're seventy-two. Lots of changes have occurred in life and society since you were a boy in Akenfield. What do you see as being the chief differences between now and then?

Class Conversation

Much of what is described in this extract from *Akenfield* is common to many people – not the external events such as the conditions in school and the work on the farm, but the feelings and thoughts that they gave rise to. Use the following questions as starting points for a class conversation on experiences of your own that may relate to what Leonard Thompson has described.

What was your first experience of working for money? What was the pay like? How did you get on with the boss?

There were a lot of hidings then. Has this form of punishment gone out of use now, or have you yourself suffered from it? Did it have the right effect?

The relationship between Leonard and his parents seemed a very good one. Why do you think it was so good? Do conditions of ordinary life, such as houses and jobs, affect the relationship between children and their parents? What difficulties can arise?

Not many children grow up without having had some kind of accident. Can you recollect any accidents or mishaps you had as a child?

Leonard wanted to get away from life in his village. Have you any wish to move to another town or district when you leave school, or are you happy to continue living where you are now?

Language

1. Leonard Thompson's speech contains many words and phrases connected with work on a farm. Find the meaning of the following:

   a bushel *a tied-cottage* *a tumbril*
   a trave or stook *a trap*

2. What would you be doing if you were: a) *pulling up docks;* b) *gleaning a field;* c) *singling mangolds?*
3. Why do you think they called the last stook 'the policeman'?
4. The style of the passage is very informal and relaxed. Leonard uses a great many colloquial phrases typical of his part of the country, such as:

   good God, what a row we made
   he changed his tune

Can you quote some more examples of colloquial expressions from the passage?

Your own writing

Some of the topics below are related to the questions you discussed in the 'Class Conversation'. Perhaps what was said then, by you yourself or by other members of the class, will help to provide material and ideas for your own writing.

1. My first job: written from your own point of view or about a character whom you create.
2. Early schooldays. Write about some of your teachers, about the conditions in the school and what you learnt there. What incidents stick in your mind from those early days?
3. If you were a keen social reformer and were living about sixty years ago, what conditions described in the passage from *Akenfield* would you want to improve?
4. Living in the country: describe a visit to a farm or a holiday in the country.
5. Getting the blame.
6. Write a short story which begins: 'The eighteen years of my life had been spent in the place where I was born. It was time I made a move and I set about planning to leave.'

Tape-recording

You may know an older person who would be willing to be interviewed about his or her early life, much as Ronald Blythe interviewed the people of Akenfield. Draw up a list of questions which will help the person you are interviewing to reminisce about the past, but allow the conversation to flow as freely and naturally as possible. Play the tape-recorded interview to the class and discuss the life-experiences that it records. You might find the following questions helpful:

Can you tell us, first, when and where you were born?
How many were there in your family?
What work did your father do?
Can you tell us something about the schools you went to?
What were the teachers like?
What did you do in the holidays?

What did you do when you left school?
Do you think life was harder then than it is now?
How did you spend your time in the evenings as a family?
Did you ever go short of anything?
What do you think of life today in comparison?

Autobiography Part One 1932–51
Adrian Henri

1

flags and bright funnels of ships
walking with my mother over the Seven Bridges
and being carried home too tired
frightened of the siren of the ferryboat
or running down the platform on the Underground
being taken over the river to see the big shops at Christmas
the road up the hill from the noisy dockyard
and the nasty smell from the tannery you didn't like going past
steep road that made your legs tired
up the hill from the Co-op the sweetshop the blue-and-white-tiled pub
Grandad's allotment on the lefthand side
behind the railings curved at the top
cobblestone path up the middle of the park
orderly rows of bean canes   a fire burning   sweetpeas tied up on
       strings

up to Our House
echoing flagyard entry between the two rows of houses
brick buttresses like lumps of cheese against the backyard walls
your feet clang and echo on the flags as you run the last few yards
pulling your woolly gloves off
shouting to show Grandad what you've just been bought
him at the door tall like the firtree in the park
darkblue suit gleaming black boots shiny silver watch chain
striped shirt no collar on but always a collarstud

heavy grey curled moustache that tickles when he picks you up to
    kiss you
sometimes shouting angry frightening you
till you see the laughter in his countryman's blue eyes

2

round redbrick doorway
yellow soapstone step cleaned twice a week
rich darkred linopattern in the polished lobby
front room with lace runners and a piano that you only go in on
    Sundays
or when someone comes to tea
Uncle Bill asleep in his chair coming in smelling of beer and horses
limping with the funny leg he got in the war
Grandma always in a flowered apron
the big green-and-red parrot frightening you with his sudden
    screeches
the two little round enamelled houses on either side of the fireplace
big turquoise flowered vase in the middle
the grate shining blackleaded cooking smell from the oven next to it

big black sooty kettle singing on the hob
fireirons in the hearth
foghorns and hooters
looking out of the kitchen window
seeing the boats on the bright river
and the cranes from the dockyards

3

coming back the taxidriver doesn't know where the street is
the allotments at the foot of the hill
gone now
great gaunt terraces of flats
scarred with graffiti
instead
the redbrick houses tiny falling apart
the whitewashed backyard
where you could smell lilyofthevalley through the privethedge
    round the tiny garden

on your way to the lavatory at the end
empty dirty overgrown now
backdoor banging in the wind
grandmother grandfather both dead in hospital
one windowpane broken dirty lace curtains flapping
the funny little flights of steps
the secret passages in the park
pink sandstone steps overhung with trees up the side of the hill
overgrown or demolished
the big seacaptain's house where I used to go for a present every
     Christmas
forgotten
remembering
lying in bed
in the dark crying listening to my mother and father argue
wind banging a shutter
indoor somewhere
dead eyes looking out from flyblown photographs
empty mirrors reflecting the silence.

Considering the poem

1. There is only one full-stop in this section from *Autobiography* and that is at the end. Why? What effect is Adrian Henri trying to create by running everything together without punctuation?
2. In the first stanza the poet suddenly begins addressing someone as 'you'. Who is he referring to? Why does he do it?
3. Adrian Henri remembers the details of childhood places and people with incredible accuracy. Which details seem to you to be particularly vivid and precise?
4. Grandfather is described with a great deal of affection. Without describing his appearance, say what sort of person you imagine him to have been.
5. What recollections does Adrian Henri have of being frightened and unhappy as a child?
6. What evidence is there in the poem to suggest that Adrian Henri approved or disapproved of the changes that had occurred in the places he knew in his childhood?

Your own writing

1. Imagine that you are ten years older and that you have been away from home for that length of time. You return to your own house and street to find that some things have changed and others have not. Describe the thoughts that go through your mind on your visit as you react to what you see and are reminded of people and incidents in the past.
2. Create a character who is revisiting a place where he has been either extremely happy or extremely unhappy – or both! What is he reminded of? What does he notice that is new? What does he feel about the place now? Is he glad to be back or does he want to get away as quickly as he can?
3. There is a strong sense of physical reality in the poem. Try to describe an interesting or unusual place you know by selecting key physical details and stringing them loosely together as Adrian Henri does to give a vivid impression of the sights, sounds and smells you have experienced.
4. What are your earliest recollections? How far back into childhood does your memory stretch? Jot down in a form similar to Adrian Henri's some of the details belonging to your earliest memories – and include a brief self-portrait.

A Confession
Jack London

It was in the evening of my last day in Reno. I had been out to the race-track watching the ponies run, and had missed my dinner (ie the mid-day meal). I was hungry, and, furthermore, a committee of public safety had just been organised to rid the town of just such hungry mortals as I. Already a lot of my brother hoboes had been gathered in by John Law, and I could hear the sunny valleys of California calling to me over the cold crests of the Sierras. Two acts remained for me to perform before I shook the dust of Reno from my feet. One was to catch the blind baggage on the west-bound overland that night. The other was first to get something to eat. Even youth will hesitate at an all-night ride, on an empty stomach, outside a train that is tearing the atmosphere through the snow-sheds, tunnels, and eternal snows of heaven-aspiring mountains.

But that something to eat was a hard proposition. I was 'turned down' at a dozen houses. Sometimes I received insulting remarks and was informed of the barred domicile that should be mine if I had my just deserts. The worst of it was that such assertions were only too true. That was why I was pulling west that night. John Law was abroad in the town, seeking eagerly for the hungry and the homeless, for by such was his barred domicile tenanted.

At other houses the doors were slammed in my face, cutting short my politely and humbly couched request for something to eat. At one house they did not open the door. I stood on the porch and knocked, and they looked out at me through the window. They even held one sturdy little boy aloft so that he could see, over the shoulders of his elders, the tramp who wasn't going to get anything to eat at their house.

I passed many houses by without venturing up to them. All houses looked alike, and none looked 'good'. After walking half a dozen blocks I shook off my despondency and gathered my 'nerve'. This begging for food was all a game, and if I didn't like the cards, I could always call for a new deal. I made up my mind to tackle the next house. I approached it in the deepening twilight, going around to the kitchen door.

I knocked softly, and when I saw the kind face of the middle-aged woman who answered, as by inspiration came to me the 'story' I was to tell. For know that upon his ability to tell a good story depends the success of the beggar. First of all, and on the instant, the beggar must 'size up' his victim. After that, he must tell a story that will appeal to the peculiar personality and temperament of that particular victim. And right here arises the great difficulty: in the instant that he is sizing up the victim he must begin his story. Not a minute is allowed for preparation. As in a lightning flash he must divine the nature of the victim and conceive a tale that will hit home. The successful hobo must be an artist. He must create spontaneously and instantaneously – and not upon a theme selected from the plenitude of his own imagination, but upon the theme he reads in the face of the person who opens the door, be it man, woman, or child, sweet or crabbed, generous or miserly, good-natured or cantankerous, Jew or Gentile, black or white, race-prejudiced or brotherly, provincial or universal, or whatever else it may be. I have often thought that to this training of my tramp days is due much of my success as a story-writer. In order to get the food whereby I lived, I was compelled to tell tales that rang true. At the back door, out of inexorable necessity, is developed the convincingness and sincerity laid down by all authorities on the art of the short-story. Also, I quite believe it was my tramp-apprenticeship that made a realist out of me. Realism constitutes the only good one can exchange at the kitchen door for grub.

But to return to the woman in Reno who opened her door to me in the deepening twilight. At the first glimpse of her kindly face I took my cue. I became a sweet, innocent, unfortunate lad. I couldn't speak. I opened my mouth and closed it again. Never in my life before had I asked anyone for food. My embarrassment was painful, extreme. I was ashamed, I, who looked upon begging as a delightful whimsicality, thumbed myself over into a true son of Mrs Grundy, burdened with all her bourgeois morality. Only the harsh pangs of belly-need could compel me to do so degraded and ignoble a thing as beg for food. And into my face I strove to throw all the wan wistfulness of famished and ingenuous youth unused to mendicancy.

'You are hungry, my poor boy,' she said.

I made her speak first.

I nodded my head and gulped.

'It is the first time I have ever . . . asked,' I faltered.

'Come right in.' The door swung open. 'We have already finished eating, but the fire is burning and I can get something up for you.'

She looked at me closely when she got me into the light.

'I wish my boy were as healthy and strong as you,' she said. 'But he is not strong. He sometimes falls down. He just fell down this afternoon and hurt himself badly, the poor dear.'

She mothered him with her voice, with an ineffable tenderness in it that I yearned to appropriate. I glanced at him. He sat across the table, slender and pale, his head swathed in bandages. He did not move, but his eyes, bright in the lamplight, were fixed upon me in a steady and wondering stare.

'Just like my poor father,' I said. 'He had the falling sickness. Some kind of vertigo. It puzzled the doctors. They never could make out what was the matter with him.'

'He is dead?' she queried gently, setting before me half a dozen soft-boiled eggs.

'Dead', I gulped. 'Two weeks ago. I was with him when it happened. We were crossing the street together. He fell right down. He was never conscious again. They carried him into a drug-store. He died there.'

And thereat I developed the pitiful tale of my father – how, after my mother's death, he and I had gone to San Fransisco from the ranch; how his pension (he was an old soldier), and the little other money he had, was not enough; and how he had tried book-canvassing. Also, I narrated my own woes during the few days after his death that I had spent alone and forlorn on the streets of San Fransisco. While that good woman warmed up biscuits, fried bacon and cooked more eggs, and while I kept pace with her in taking care of all that she placed before me, I enlarged the picture of that poor orphan boy and filled in the details. I became that poor boy. I believed in him as I believed in the beautiful eggs I was devouring. I could have wept for myself, I know the tears did get into my voice at times. It was very effective.

In fact, with every touch I added to the picture, that kind soul gave me something also. She made up a lunch for me to carry away. She put in many boiled eggs, pepper and salt, and other things, and a big apple. She provided me with three pairs of thick red woollen socks. She gave me clean handkerchiefs and other things which I have since forgotten. And all the time she cooked more and more and I ate more and more. I gorged like a savage; but then it was a far cry across the Sierras on a blind baggage, and I knew not when nor where I should find my next meal. And all the while, like a death's head at the feast, silent and motionless, her unfortunate boy sat and stared at me across the table. I suppose I represented to him mystery, and romance, and adventure – all that was denied the feeble flicker of life that was in him. And yet I could not forbear, once or twice, from wondering if he saw through me down to the bottom of my mendacious heart.

'But where are you going to?' she asked me.

'Salt Lake City,' said I. 'I have a sister there – a married sister.' (I debated if I should make a Mormon out of her and decided against it.) 'Her husband is a plumber – a contracting plumber.'

Now I knew that contracting plumbers were usually credited with making lots of money. But I had spoken. It was up to me to qualify.

'They would have sent me the money for my fare if I had asked for it,' I explained, 'but they have had sickness and business troubles. His partner cheated him. And so I wouldn't write for the money. I knew I could make my way there somehow. I let them think I had enough to get me to Salt Lake City. She is lovely, and so kind to me. I guess I'll go into the shop and learn the trade. She has two daughters. They are younger than I. One is only a baby.'

Of all my married sisters that I have distributed among the cities of the United States, the Salt Lake sister is my favourite, She is quite real, too. When I tell about her, I can see her, and her two little girls, and her plumbing husband. She is a large, motherly woman, just verging on beneficent stoutness – the kind, you know, that always cooks nice things and that never gets angry. She is a brunette. Her husband is a quiet, easy-going fellow. Sometimes I almost know him quite well. And who knows but some day I may meet him.

On the other hand, I have a feeling of certitude within me that I shall never meet in the flesh my many parents and grandparents –

you see, I invariably killed them off. Heart disease was my favourite way of getting rid of my mother, though on occasion I did away with her by means of consumption, pneumonia, and typhoid fever. It is true, as the Winnipeg policemen will attest, that I have grandparents living in England; but that was a long time ago and it is a fair assumption that they are dead now. At any rate, they have never written to me.

I hope that woman in Reno will read these lines and forgive me my gracelessness and unveracity. I do not apologise, for I am unashamed. It was youth, delight in life, zest for experience, that brought me to her door. It did me good. It taught me the intrinsic kindliness of human nature. I hope it did her good. Anyway, she may get a good laugh out of it now that she learns the real inwardness of the situation.

To her my story was 'true'. She believed in me and all my family, and she was filled with solicitude for the dangerous journey I must make ere I won to Salt Lake City. This solicitude nearly brought me to grief. Just as I was leaving, my arms full of lunch and my pockets bulging with fat woollen socks, she bethought herself of a nephew, or uncle, or relative of some sort, who was in the railway mail service, and who, moreover, would come through that night on the very train on which I was going to steal my ride. The very thing! She would take me down to the depot, tell him my story, and get him to hide me in the mail car. Thus, without danger or hardship, I would be carried straight through to Ogden. Salt Lake City was only a few miles farther on. My heart sank. She grew excited as she developed the plan and with sinking heart I had to feign unbounded gladness at this solution of my difficulties.

Solution! Why, I was bound west that night, and here was I being trapped into going east. It *was* a trap, and I hadn't the heart to tell her that it was all a miserable lie. And while I made believe that I was delighted, I was busy cudgelling my brains for some way to escape. But there was no way. She would see me into the mail-car – she said so herself – and then that mail-clerk relative of hers would carry me to Ogden. And then I would have to beat my way back over all those hundreds of miles of desert.

But luck was with me that night. Just about the time she was getting ready to put on her bonnet and accompany me, she discovered that she had made a mistake. Her mail-clerk relative was not scheduled to come through that night. His run had been changed.

He would not come through until two nights afterwards. I was saved, for, of course my boundless youth would never permit me to wait those two days. I optimistically assured her that I'd get to Salt Lake City quicker if I started immediately, and I departed with her blessings and best wishes ringing in my ears.

But those woollen socks were great. I know. I wore a pair of them that night on the blind baggage of the overland, and that overland went west.

(adapted from *Confession*)

The Interview

Imagine that you are the author, Jack London, and that you are being interviewed. Write down what you would say in answer to these questions. Don't reply too briefly – develop what you have to say as fully as you can.

1. What do you mean when you say, *this begging for food was all a game, and if I didn't like the cards, I could always call for a new deal*? What 'new deal' could you have called for?
2. We normally condemn lying as being wrong, yet you lied shamelessly to the woman. How do you justify yourself?
3. As you say, you have to be a good judge of character when you are inventing a story. What did you decide about this woman's character when your first saw her?
4. Why do you think she was so kind and took such a liking to you? Had her son anything to do with it?
5. You call this piece of writing 'Confession'. Why do you feel you ought to confess?
6. What do you think the woman would say now if she read your confession?
7. You didn't have to beg. You say it was *youth, delight in life, zest for experience* that made you do it. What were these delights and what would you say you gained from the experience?
8. I can't believe that if the relative had turned up on the through-train you would have gone with him to Salt Lake City! You could surely have talked your way out of that one! What story would you have made up if the woman had insisted on taking you to the mail-car?

Class Conversation

There are many kinds of 'truth' and many kinds of 'lies'. How much
'truth' is there in each of the following statements?
    There are seven days in one week.
    The sun rises in the east and sets in the west.
    Kippers taste horrible!
    My love is like a red, red rose.
    I always tell lies.
    It's a free country.
    I promise to tell the truth, the whole truth and nothing but the
    truth.

Do you think it is true that everyone tells lies in some form or other?
Do you tell lies then?
Did lying ever get you into trouble? Or were your lies 'successful'?

Can you suggest reasons why each of the following might, in certain
circumstances, avoid telling the plain truth?
    a doctor   a salesman   a politician   a teacher   a parent
    a witness at a trial   a school pupil

Why do people lie about their age?
Have you ever lied about your age?

Have you ever gone from door to door trying to sell something? Did
you find it easy or difficult, enjoyable or not? How successful were
you?
Looking at it from the other side of the door: what callers have you
had at your house recently? What was your attitude towards them?

Have you ever done anything for people who are less well-off than
yourself?
Have you ever taken part in an event sponsored for charity? What
did you think of your experience?

Acting

In pairs or in small groups, prepare and produce sketches on the
theme of 'excuses', using the following situations:

arriving late for school
turning up at games or P.E. without kit
failing to hand in homework
getting home very late one night
leaving a supermarket with goods you haven't paid for
committing a parking offence
travelling on a bus or a train without a ticket

Develop a scene in which the young Jack London has his *politely and humbly couched request for something to eat* rejected with appropriately insulting remarks from the person who comes to the door.

Scene: at the front door of a house. Characters: a caller and one or two members of the family. Situations:
a Christmas tip for the newspaper boy or girl
collecting jumble
selling raffle tickets or fête programmes
a gipsy selling pegs, bags of lavender, etc.
signatures for a petition on a controversial subject affecting your town
a mysterious night caller.

Word-study

Have a dictionary handy for this part of the work.

1. What is a 'mortal'? (page 13, line 5.) What is its opposite? What other words beginning with *mort* are connected in meaning with death?
2. Who is Jack London referring to when he speaks of *John Law*? (page 13, line 6)
3. What is meant by the phrase *heaven-aspiring mountains*? (page 13, line 13)
4. What, in simpler language, would the *barred domicile* be? (page 13, line 16)
5. If a person gets his *just deserts* (page 13, line 17) what does he get?
6. What is meant by the word 'divine' in the phrase *divine the nature of the victim*? (page 14, line 16.) What other meaning has this word?

7. What is a Gentile?
8. Who was Mrs Grundy?
9. 'Bourgeois' refers to a particular class in society. Which class? What other names are used to describe social classes?
10. 'Ingenuous' means 'simple, innocent, sincere'. What prefix would you add to the word to make it the opposite, meaning 'cunning, deceitful, sly'?
11. 'Appropriate' here means 'to take over, to acquire'. What other meaning does the word have? What is its opposite?
12. Find the following words in the text and write them down in a column:
    couched   plenitude   cantankerous   ignoble   wan   mendicancy   vertigo   beneficent   mendacious   solicitude
    Opposite each word put a word from the group below that has almost the same meaning:
    mean   expressed   begging   fullness   lying   quarrelsome   giddiness   pale   concern   kind

Your own writing

1. Jack London took to begging because he wanted to see what it was like – he had what he called a *zest for experience*. Imagine that you have decided to seek a completely new experience in life, quite different from anything you have met with so far. Describe how you found your new experience and whether or not it turned out to be successful.
2. There have been instances of men arranging their disappearance and apparent death and then assuming a new identity – usually in a foreign country – by forging papers and a passport. Can you use the idea of a 'disappearance' as the basis of a story in which a man has to change his identity?
3. Jack London was expert at inventing fantastic stories about imaginary parents and relatives. Do the same yourself. Invent a fantastic life-story for a fictitious relative – and try to believe in it yourself as you write it!
4. Write the continuation of a story which begins: 'I went to the next house, which, I thought, looked more promising than the last one. I knocked on the door and waited. No answer. I knocked again. Still no answer. I was about to walk away when

I heard a noise inside the house and the door opened about two inches . . .

5. A good short story, says Jack London, should be convincing and sincere. Write a good short story based on an incident that happened in your own life or in the life of someone you know. It need not be absolutely true, for you will need to 'shape' it a little to make it more effective, but it should sound true when it is read.

6. Are you in favour of sponsored charity events, such as walks, swims, silences, fasts etc? Give the arguments for and against helping charities in this way.
   Or: write an account of your own part in a sponsored event.

7. Write a short play, an essay or a story on one of the topics discussed in 'Class Conversation'.

Alex at the Barber's
John Fuller

He is having his hair cut. Towels are tucked
About his chin, his mop scalped jokingly.
The face in the mirror is his own face.

The barber moves and chats among the green
And methylated violet, snipper-snips,
Puts scissors down, plugs in a plaited flex,

And like a surgeon with his perfumed hands
Presses the waiting skull and shapes the base.
He likes having his hair cut, and the man

Likes cutting it. The radio drones on.
The eyes in the mirror are his own eyes.
While the next chair receives the Demon Blade,

A dog-leg razor nicks a sideburn here;
As from a sofa there a sheet is whisked
And silver pocketed. The doorbell pings.

The barber, frowning, grips the ragged fringe
And slowly cuts. Upon the speckled sheet
The bits fall down and now his hair is cut.

The neighing trams outside splash through the rain.
The barber tests the spray for heat and rubs
Lemon shampoo into his spiky hair.

Bent with his head above the running bowl,
Eyes squeezed shut, he does not see the water
Gurgle and sway like twisted sweetpaper

Above the waste, but, for a moment, tows
A sleigh of polished silver parrots through
Acres of snow, exclaiming soundlessly.

Then towel round head. Head swung gently up.
Eyes padded. As the barber briskly rubs,
The smile in the mirror is his own smile.

Considering the poem

1. The form of the poem is very simple: three unrhymed lines to
   each verse. The content is familiar. It is a description, with
   some excellent detail, of what happens in a typical barber's
   shop. The actions of the barber are well observed: he tucks the
   towels about the boy's chin . . . he *moves and chats* . . . *puts
   scissors down.* Can you continue this list of actions by quoting
   short phrases from the poem?
2. Several articles in the shop are mentioned. Can you give some
   examples?
3. Where in the poem are there echoes of the third line?
4. The poem becomes a little more difficult in the ninth verse. Can
   you explain it?

Your own experience

Describe in poetry or in prose a similar experience of your own, such
as being fitted for new clothes, having a tooth taken out, undergoing
a medical examination – or simply going to the barber's or hairdres-
ser's. Include some well-observed detail in your writing.

Childhood Agonies
Catherine Cookson

Catherine Cookson was brought up in East Jarrow by her unmarried mother ('Our Kate') in the home of her grandparents. The family's poverty brought young Katie more than her fair share of suffering and humiliation.

Then there was the business of being late. It was quite a walk from East Jarrow to Tyne Dock School. And I was almost as bad at getting up in the morning as me Uncle Jack. Often I was running the last few yards past the church, taking the short cut up the wall where the children's feet had carved out steps over the years, and into the playground, just too late. The bell had gone, and the last of the crocodiles had disappeared into their classrooms. And there we would be, the latecomers. I had just . . . just missed getting in by a matter of seconds. I would tell them so, and keep saying it to anyone who would listen. Then in the middle of its protest my voice would be silenced by the overpowering feeling of dread descending on me. Sometimes we had to stand fifteen minutes for her coming. And those fifteen minutes were like years full of agony. Down the waiting line the boys would be spitting on their hands and rubbing them on their breeches, which was supposed to toughen the skin. I, like most of the other girls, would be standing by now with my legs crossed doing a kind of minor St. Vitus Dance. Very often the dance became reality, for when your hands were frozen and that cane swished through the air and split them in two you left the ground and jangled out animal sounds.

I became so terrified of this woman that I began a snivelling, placating campaign. I would go to Mrs. Dixon's at Simonside, mostly on a Monday morning, and there with a penny I had kept hidden for the purpose I would get a penn'orth of flowers, and a big bunch at that. These were for Miss Corfield. Very often because I would stand talking to Mrs Dixon I would be late and Miss Corfield would take the flowers from my hand, lay them aside, then say, 'Hold your hand out.'

I remember hugging a great old book to school. It was about two feet high and four inches thick and bound in warm leather. Kate had seen this book lying on a side table in a butcher's shop in Leygate. The butcher was going to tear it up for wrapping. It was full of old illustrations of London and she asked him for it and brought it home. A great value was put on this book in the kitchen, the pictures were so old, so I asked if I could take it to school to show Miss Corfield. I remember going to her with it, but what happened I don't know. I next see myself waiting at dinnertime outside the gate and walking with her towards her house above the station, trying to open this huge tome as I went along to show her the pictures. All to no avail. I came home from school one day and said, 'Miss Corfield says we've all got to take three yards of flannelette to make a nightie.' Kate made no reply. They were all out of work at the time. A month later: 'Our Kate, Miss Corfield says, if I don't bring the flannelette I'll get wrong. I've kept on tellin' you for weeks I've got to take the flannelette.'

It was on a Friday night when I started again and I kept on all day on the Saturday for I was petrified of going to school on the Monday morning without the material.

Around tea time she suddenly burst out, 'All right, I'll get you the blasted flannelette. Come on.'

She took me into Jarrow. We walked all the way in the dark. I don't remember to which shop we went, but I do remember that my eyes nearly sprang from their sockets when I saw her pick up part of a bale of flannelette that was standing on display in the shop doorway and walk away with it. I scrambled after her into the back lane where she pushed it up under her coat, and then we both ran. I remember coming round by the lonely Quay corner and her having to stop because I was sick. I retched and retched, and when she got indoors she retched too.

I took a piece of the flannelette to school on the Monday. It was cut out into a nightdress, and when I left three years later it was still there, unfinished.

The kitchen was the hub of my life; it was the centre of the universe from which all pain and pleasure sprang. In it would be enacted battles both physical and mental. One particular battle happened at least once a week between Kate and myself. It would begin with her saying 'I don't want you to go to school this mornin'.' This should have filled me with joy but it didn't. For it meant only one thing, she wanted me to go to the pawn. I would stand nearly always at the kitchen door leading into the scullery, from which you went by another door into the backyard. I would take up this position as if ready for flight. She would not look at me as she told me why she would have to send me to the pawn but would go about her business of clearing a table, or preparing food, or lifting up the mats, or throwing a great bucket of slack to the back of the fireplace in preparation for the tea leaves that would be put on it to clag it together. And she would be saying, 'It's the rent, I've just got to have it. This is the second week and they could put us in Court.' Being taken to Court had the same horror for her as the workhouse had for me granda. She would not have been 'put in Court' for two weeks rent, but there were outstanding arrears of something between four and five pounds, and as the rent was only about four and six a week they represented many unpaid weeks. Her debts hung over her head like an avalanche about to plunge down and bury her. Yet the irony was that if they had all kept off the drink for a few weeks the debts would have been cleared and she would have been without that particular worry. But people with Kate's weakness don't reason. They can only satisfy the craving in their stomachs, and answer censure with, 'Well, what else have I got?'

From my position by the door I would say, 'I'm not going, our Kate.' She would remain silent, moving swiftly from one place in the room to another. My eyes would follow her and when she didn't answer I would go on, 'I hate going. It's awful. Everybody looks at me. I'm not going, do you hear?'

Sometimes she would suddenly stop in her darting and sit down and rest her head in her hands. This would be too much for me. I would bow my own head and step into the room and wait. But at other times she would turn on me, crying, 'You'll do what you're damn well told. Now get your hat and jacket on and get away.'

Sometimes I would stand and watch her as she parcelled up the things. Very often they were just bits of underwear still damp from the wash. Sometimes it might be a suit, me Uncle Jack's suit, never me granda's. I never knew him to have a suit or anything worth pawning, until I was fourteen or so. Sometimes she would go to the drawer and take out her blouse, her only decent blouse, and there I would stand watching her parcelling the things up while she said, 'Ask him to stretch a point and make it five shillings,' knowing as she said this that I'd be lucky if I returned with three.

I would go out of the front door with the parcel and nearly always there'd be somebody in the street doing their step or their windows, and they'd know where I was going. But this was nothing; the real agony started when I reached the bottom of the dock bank, for the dock bank was always lined with men, waiting to be signed on for work. They would all be standing against the dock offices and the railings that led up to the little photographic shop where the road divided, the right hand section leading up to Stanhope Road, the left going to the station and The Crown. But opposite to where the men stood the streets went off at right angles, Dock Street, Bede Street, Hudson Street. Gompertz the pawnshop, known as Bob's, was situated in Bede Street. To get to it I had to pass the gauntlet of men. They all knew who I was. I wasn't known as Kate's daughter, but old John's grand-bairn. Nearly always opposite Bede Street, among the men, would be standing Black Charlie. He was a negro and, I understand, an interpreter. Yet he lived in Bede Street with his black wife and black children. They were a happy and good family and the children went to Tyne Dock School.

How do you assess the agonies of childhood? How do you go about putting them over? There is no way to measure these agonies. As an adult you can translate pain into description; you can describe the effects of some particular hurt whether mental or physical. But as a child you have as yet acquired no words to fit the pain. Even if you had you wouldn't be capable of applying them to your particular torments. All you can do as a child is feel and protest through tears. Should you struggle to translate your feelings all you can convey is that you are frightened, or that you've got a pain, or that you don't like this or that, and you can cry as you say this, or bash out, but nothing you can do at that age had the power to convey the feeling of being buried under a tremendous weight of fear, of humiliation and shame.

But I was going up Hudson Street to the pawn. To avoid the eyes of the waiting men I would often hang on to a ha'penny in order to take the tram from the Dock Gates to the station, just two stops up. This was the Shields tram. I wasn't known to anyone on this tram. I imagined when the men saw me getting on to the tram they wouldn't think I was going to the pawn. I would get off at the station, go up the slope and down the steps and past The Crown, to which I joyfully escaped on a Saturday afternoon, and make by way down Bede Street back lane. I would go in the back yard of Bob's shop, then through the passage where the pawning cubicles were. But I never went in these, that would have been the last straw. No, I went out now into the front street, turning my back on the men standing facing the bottom of it. Then I would look in Bob's shop windows. In one side he had an assortment of watches and jewellery. In the other was a show of clothes, mostly moleskin trousers, blue-striped shirts, so stiff they would stand up by themselves, and great sailors' boots. When I had let myself be observed long enough to prove to all concerned that I was going in to buy something, I would open the door and step down into the dark well of Bob's shop. Sometimes, even when in the shop, I carried the pretence still further. To the right hand side was a bench on which was a conglomeration of garments from unredeemed pledges. Among these I would sort as if looking for something to buy. The pretence would be rent apart when Bob would say, 'Well, what is it, hinny?'

With my voice very humble I would answer, 'Kate says can she have five shillings on these?'

He would open the parcel and sort out the things, making comments perhaps on a garment, saying, 'Well, this has seen its last days, hinny, hasn't it . . . and that's not worth tuppence. I'm sorry, lass, but the most I can give you is half-a-crown.'

I would just stare at him and he would repeat 'I'm sorry.' Then he would walk away into the back shop and there would follow a period of waiting, for I was well under age and according to law a person under fourteen could not put in a pledge.

Sometimes I hadn't to wait long and a woman would come into a cubicle and he would say to her, 'I've got a bairn here, will you put it in for her?'

He was a kind man was Bob, an understanding man. I look back upon him with affection, for he must have realised how I felt about this business. He knew all my tricks but never alluded to them, and he always did the asking for me. If the woman was in the shop when he asked her I wouldn't look at her. Yet if I got over five shillings I would hand her tuppence for signing the ticket. If I got under five shillings I would give her a penny.

All the times I went to Bob's I never saw a child of my own age there, nor yet a man, other than Bob himself.

I had been going to the pawn for some years and was about eleven I think when I asked myself, 'Why can't our Kate go herself?' and it came to me that she was as ashamed as I was to be seen going to the pawn. She didn't want to run the gauntlet of eyes either. And this was the reason why when I couldn't be kept off school to go to Bob's – perhaps the board man had paid one of his frequent visits only a day or so before – I was sent on almost equally painful borrowing excursions. Anything to save her having to run the gauntlet.

But these weren't the only bad mornings. There were mornings when I had to go across to Mrs. Flanagan's in Philipson Street and ask for the loan of a suit.

Mrs. Flanagan was a good friend to Kate and Kate in her turn repaid her with hard work, but she did things for Kate that others would not have done, like lending her Mr. Flanagan's suit to pawn. Mrs. Flanagan was a nice small timid looking little woman, always ailing, and I felt sorry for her, except when I had to go and ask her if she would lend Kate Mr. Flanagan's suit to take to the pawn. In these moments I hated her, I hated her for existing, I hated her for having a man who had a suit that was pawnable. But Mr. Flanagan had not only one suit, he had a number of suits. He was a man who saw to number one.

(from *Our Kate*)

The Interview

Answer the questions as though you were the author being interviewed. Develop your replies as fully as you can, basing them on your understanding of the passage.

1. Do you think Miss Corfield was right in refusing to be influenced by the flowers you took her? After all, she wasn't going to be bribed, was she?
2. I can't imagine the incident of the flannelette happening these days, can you?
3. What do you see as being the essential difference between the

way an adult expresses his feelings of pain and unhappiness
and the way a child expresses them?
4. As a child you were sensitive to the opinions of others about you
– particularly the men at the dock bank when you were going to
the pawn. Looking back, what do you think the men really
thought of you?
5. When you looked in the window and pretended to be choosing
something to buy, do you think you were deceiving anyone?
Wasn't it all in your imagination what others would think of
you?
6. Why weren't you embarrassed in front of Bob?
7. You were very poor, yet you gave a tip to the woman who put
the clothes in pawn for you. What made you do that?
8. You felt resentful at that time, when Kate made you do what
she herself was unwilling to do. Are you still resentful, or do
you think now she was justified?
9. Would you agree that you were a rather complex child? Can you
understand now why you felt and behaved as you did in those
days?

Talking about ourselves

Catherine Cookson, like most of us, was concerned about what other
people thought of her. In what kind of situation are you self-
conscious about what people will think or say about you?

Do you recognise Katie's resentment at being made to go to the
pawnshop? Most children, at some time or other, are made to do
what they don't want to do – particularly by parents! Any examples?

Katie took things to the pawn when she was under-age. Are you
always on the right side of the 'under-age' laws?

The 'agonies of childhood' described in the passage relate particularly to the fear of the teacher and the shame of being poor. There
are many other agonies, of course. What would you say your particular agony was?

Think about your experience of going into shops to buy things. How
do you react to the shopkeeper, the sales assistant or the check-out

person? Are you (and they) usually polite? What causes argument and ill feeling?

Shop-lifting is becoming increasingly common, especially in self-service stores. Not many adults can honestly claim never to have 'pinched' something in their childhood. Who'll be the first to confess?

Miss Corfield seemed to show very little sympathy for Katie's problems. Is your experience that teachers are often insensitive to the needs of their pupils? Or do they usually show real understanding? On what occasions have you been either misjudged or positively helped by teachers?

Word-study

1. Several of the words and phrases used in the passage are Tyneside dialect. Using 'our' and 'me' before names ('our Kate' and 'me granda' for instance) is common in the North when speaking of close members of the family. Find the following dialect expressions in the passage and give an equivalent meaning for each:
   I'll get wrong (page 26, line 24), *slack* (page 27, line 15), *clag* (page 27, line 16, *grand-bairn* (page 28, line 23), *hinny* (page 29, line 24), *who saw to number one* (page 30, line 26).

2. Explain the meaning of the following words and phrases:
   St. Vitus Dance (page 25, line 21), *a placating campaign* (page 26, line 2), *this huge to me* (page 26, line 19), *put in Court* (page 27, line 20), *unredeemed pledges* (page 29, line 22), *alluded to* (page 29, line 40), *run the gauntlet* (page 30, line 10), *the board man* (page 30, line 12).

3. Collect some examples of your local dialect.

Tape-recording

How do people speak in your town or district? Is there a local dialect or accent? Are there variations in speech within a small area? Do some research! Tape-record a number of separate interviews with local people and try to answer the questions: Who are the most effective speakers? What interesting expressions are used that are typical of your part of the country? What differences in accent are there? What influence have age, education, occupation and place of birth on the way people speak? Is there a 'right' and a 'wrong' way to speak English?

It might be tricky getting some of your speakers started. These questions could help you:

Do you know what a pawnshop is? Have you ever seen one?
Has this area changed much since you first knew it?
Did you enjoy school when you were young?
Can you describe one or two of your teachers?
What was the best holiday you ever had?
What have you done today?

Role-play

Members of the class are asked to represent the main characters from the passage: Katie, Kate, Miss Corfield, Bob, Mrs. Flanagan and, perhaps a worker from the dock bank. They sit at the front of the class in turn and answer questions put to them by the rest of the class. The question we are seeking an answer to is: was Katie's suffering her own fault, or were other people responsible for it? Katie might be asked why she didn't tell Miss Corfield that she couldn't afford the flannelette. Miss Corfield might be asked why she insisted on it in the first place. The worker could be asked whether he ever noticed Katie going to the pawn – and whether he thought anything of it. Probe as deeply as you can into the actions of the characters.

Sketches

Re-read the account of Katie's going to the pawnshop, then either write or improvise a short sketch based upon it, using, if you wish, the following outline:

Scene: inside the pawnshop. A counter and a bench to the right of it on which is a pile of unredeemed clothes. Katie enters and looks at the articles on the bench.

Conversation between Bob and Katie.

Bob goes into the back shop. A woman customer enters the shop with articles to pawn. Bob enters to serve her.

Conversation between customer and Bob in which he asks her to 'put

in' the articles for Katie. Katie is given the money, then offers a penny to the woman. Katie goes out. Bob and the woman discuss her.
Do not use only the conversation in the passage. Make up your own dialogue and develop the characters and situation as fully as you can.

Re-read the part beginning *The kitchen was the hub of my life* and ending, *I'd be lucky if I returned with three.* Write or improvise a sketch on what is described in this passage.

Prepare a sketch set in a shop of any kind. The characters are the shop owner or an assistant and one or two customers. There is an argument, an attempt at theft, a misunderstanding over payment, a complaint, or simply a pleasant chat about this and that. Develop your sketch humorously or dramatically and try to create some interesting characters.

Your own writing

Choose one of the subjects below or any of the topics in 'Talking about ourselves' for your composition.

1. Money – or the shortage of it – was responsible for much of the suffering described in the extract from *Our Kate*. Take an individual, either imaginary or of your own acquaintance (for instance, a mother, a wife, a pensioner, a teenager, a rich 'star', or yourself) and in the form of a story or an essay write about his or her problems with money.
2. Your title is: 'What will they think of me?' Imagine you are a person in a special position – perhaps a football star, a singer, an actor, an important speaker, a new teacher, a young bride – who is going to be in the public eye. Write down the thoughts of the person before, during and after the event.
3. Poverty today. Where does it exist? How do people cope? What examples can you give? What more needs to be done to alleviate poverty?
4. The shoplifter.
5. Choose a character who is unemployed. Describe a typical day in his life and allow him to express his thoughts about his situation and what the future might hold.

Family Group
Ken Smith

He also was a stormy day: a squat mountain man
smelling of sheep and the high pasture, stumping
through pinewoods, hunched and small, feeling
the weather on him. Work angled him.
Fingers were crooked with frost, stiffened.

Ploughing, he would fix his eye on the hawthorn,
walking firm booted, concerned for the furrow.
Horse and man in motion together, deliberate,
one foot put before the other, treading out clay.
He would not see the bird perched on the plough.
He would not chase the plover limping over the stubble.

He was my father who brought in wood and lit
the hissing lamp. And he would sit, quiet
as moor, before the fire. She drew him
slowly out of silence. She had a coat
made from a blanket and wore boy's shoes.
She was small and had red hands, firm boned,
and her hair was greying. The house was stone
and slate. It was her house, his home,
and their family; and they quarrelled often.

She churned butter, baked and scrubbed floors,
and for twenty years he laboured the raw earth
and rough weather. In winter we made mats

from rags with pegs. We guarded ourselves,
and were close. We were poor, and poorer banking
every safe pound. Each year passed slowly.

Now he lives in the glass world of his shop,
and time is grudged. Ham and tinned meat
and vegetables are his breathing day.
He works harder and is unhappy. She too
stoops through the labouring year, is greyer,
and grumbles. Nothing is made any more
but money, that cannot be made. Nothing
means happiness. The light comes down wires,
water through tubes. All is expensive, paid.

Silence is gone from their lives; the city
has taken all that poised energy. Violence
is articulate. The deliberate motion is gone,
and he moves with pain through time that is work
that is cash. He will not notice the crashed
gull fallen in the storm, the grabbing sparrow.
She cannot tease him into speech, or be content
before the broody fire. She is in fashion now.
But seasons pass them without touching.
They will not feel the winter when it comes.

Considering the poem

1. There are several contrasts in the poem, showing the changes
   that came over Ken Smith's parents when they moved from the
   mountain farm to the shop in the city. Can you find expressions
   in the first four stanzas to correspond with these quotations
   from the final stanzas?
   a) time is grudged
   b) Nothing is made any more
   c) The light comes down wires
   d) The deliberate motion is gone
   *e) She cannot tease him into speech, or be content before the
   broody fire.*
   f) She is in fashion now.

2. What other contrasts in their lives can you find?
3. Why does Ken Smith see life on the farm as being better than life in the city?
4. Why do you think the family decided to make the move?

Talking or writing

If you decide to write, you could choose to write in the form of a poem, a short story or an essay.

1. Moving from one place to another: what changes were there in physical surroundings and in the lives of the people you are writing about? Was the move a change for the better or the worse?
2. Referring to your own experience as much as possible, compare living:
    in the country and in a town or city;
    or by the sea and inland;
    or abroad and in this country;
    or in two different kinds of dwelling.
    Consider the way people are affected by the places they live in.
3. The countryman's relationship with animals and with nature can be fundamentally different from the town dweller's. One may use animals for work or see them as pests to be killed, the other may keep them as pets or use them in sport; one may be out in all weathers, the other may spend most of his day in a factory or an office. Write about these differences in any way you choose. You might like to create two characters who talk to each other about their respective attitudes towards animals and nature.

First Climb
Christian Bonington

Christian Bonington describes how, as a schoolboy, he set off with a friend to climb Snowdon and having enjoyed his first taste of mountaineering he looked for ways in which his interest could be developed. From these beginnings he eventually became the leader of the British expedition which, in 1976, climbed Everest 'the hard way'.

Once back at school, I started to put my dreams into practice; the first thing was to find someone to share my enthusiasm. Shortly before Christmas I persuaded one of my form-mates to join me in an expedition to Wales. We set out just after Christmas and hitch-hiked up to Snowdonia. Anton had only his shoes to walk in, while I had brought a pair of ex-army boots that had a few studs in the soles. We had no windproofs, but relied on our school burberries.

We had chosen one of the hardest winters of recent years for our introduction to the hills. There was barely any traffic on the road and we spent the entire day getting from Llangollen, near the Welsh border, to Capel Curig in the heart of Snowdonia, but this did not matter, it was all so new and exciting; even the walks between lifts were enjoyable, as the country got progressively more bleak and wild and the hills got higher. Just as it grew dark we reached Capel Curig. There are few views to beat that of Snowdon from Capel, especially when the mountains are covered with snow. The three peaks of the Snowdon Horse Shoe stood isolated a good seven miles away, but in the crisp, clear air it seemed even farther. They had all the grandeur of Himalayan giants, yet were within our grasp.

That night in the youth hostel Anton and I made our plans. We had not the faintest idea of what mountaineering would entail, and looking round the common-room at all the confident, experienced climbers, I felt very green. We sat huddled in a corner, very conscious of our complete ignorance and the fact that we did not look the part, that we had none of the right clothes. I longed for a pair of proper climbing boots with plenty of nails in the soles, or real climbing breeches and a well darned sweater.

The conversation for the most part was in climbing jargon that was difficult to understand, everyone talking at the top of his voice about the day's exploits, and, as far as one could see, no-one really listening. A big, bearded man with a hole in the seat of his camouflaged ex-army windproofs was sitting immediately behind us and was describing, with a wealth of gestures, a narrow escape that day.

'The ice was at least eighty degrees with an inch of powder snow on top. I'd run out sixty feet without a runner and Roy only had an axe belay. Near the top it got even steeper and turned to black ice. There was only an inch of it and you hit rock. It was all I could do to get up it.'

I couldn't really understand what he was talking about, though it sounded most impressive. I was much too shy to talk to anyone, but just sat in a corner and listened. I looked ridiculously young for my age anyway; though I was nearly six foot tall and of average build, I had a fresh complexion and smooth skin that made me look little more than fourteen. I was always intensely aware of this, and this as much as anything made me shy and tongue-tied at first in the company of strangers.

We had a map, and there was a path marked all the way up Snowdon from Pen y Pass, so we decided to follow it the next day. We did not like consulting anyone about our plans, but if we had done, I am sure we should have been warned off Snowdon, for in severe winter conditions even the easiest way up can be dangerous and has claimed many lives. The next morning, happily ignorant, we hitch-hiked to Pen y Pass, just below Crib Goch. The path, marked on our maps, ran along the side of the ridge above the deeply glaciated cwm of Glas Llyn, but standing by the roadside it did not seem to be much help. The weather had changed overnight; the cloud was down and it was beginning to snow. From the road, the white of the snow, broken only by black gashes of exposed rocks, merged imperceptibly with the clouds. There were a few tracks in the snow, but whether these were the paths marked on the map, who could tell?

We were about to turn back when a group of three climbers, who looked very professional with their ice-axes and windproofs, strode past and plunged into the snow. We followed them; soon we had not the faintest idea where we were as the snow swirled around us and we floundered up to our waists in it. My feet quickly lost all sense of feeling, it was so cold. Anton was in an even worse state without proper boots, and continually slipping. The figures in front were vague blurs in the rushing snow; above us loomed black cliffs, below, the steeply dropping white slope merged into the cloud and only occasionally could we see the dull black surface of Glas Llyn through a momentary break. We ended up in a minor avalanche when we must have been quite high on the slopes of Crib Goch. Suddenly, everything around us was moving and we rolled and slid in a steadily moving chute of snow down the slope. We had no real comprehension of danger and arrived at the bottom laughing. If there had been a cliff on the way down we could have been seriously injured. The people we had followed had not had any more sense than us and had floundered about in the soft snow just as incompetently. I returned to the hostel that night soaked to the skin, exhausted, but completely happy – it was the most exciting and enjoyable day I had ever had. Anton did not share my enthusiasm; he returned to London the next day and never came back to the hills. I stayed on by myself for a few more days. For the most part I kept to the roads and walked from one youth hostel to the next, but I could never pluck up courage to talk to anyone in the evenings until my last night. The youth hostel at Capel Curig was full and so I found a little bed-and-breakfast place to spend the night in. Two climbers arrived just as it got dark and we spent the evening together. It was easy to talk to them, to find out something about real rock climbing, and what they told me confirmed my ambition to be a climber.

Back at school I dreamt of the mountains and of rock climbing. I read every book I could lay my hands on. But the real problem was to find someone to climb with. In Wales I had seen the danger of solitary wandering and, anyway, wanted to climb properly with a rope. Today, even in the last twelve years, climbing has expanded out of all recognition: in London there are many local clubs, all of which encourage beginners and welcome new members; there are organisations such as the Mountaineering Association and the Central Council of Physical Recreation, that organise training courses, so that it is not too difficult to learn how to climb. In 1951, however, there were few local clubs anywhere and none in London. No one at school was interested in the mountains and there seemed no way of finding anyone to teach me to climb.

Finally, I ran down a friend of the family who had done some climbing. He agreed to take me down to Harrison's Rocks, an outcrop in Kent only forty miles south of London. It seemed incredible that there could be crags so close to the city in Southern England. I had always associated climbing with the bleak hills of Scotland and Wales, certainly not with the hop fields of Kent. I met Cliff one Sunday morning at the end of March on Victoria Station. I had an irrational feeling of superiority over all the thousands of other travellers who were merely going down to the coast for a day by the sea and was intensely conscious of the length of old hemp rope in my rucksack; I longed to take it out and sling it round my shoulder, but felt too self-conscious to do so. We were not the only mountaineers travelling down to Tunbridge Wells – you could tell them from the patches in their trousers and the battered anoraks. We all piled out of the train at Groombridge and walked up an ordinary country road. There was still no sign of any rocks, even when we went through a wood of young trees; and then, suddenly, we came to the top of a sandstone cliff. It was only thirty feet high; the trees growing at its base towered above its crest; a railway ran along the bed of the valley through fields of hops and past an oast house. I could not help being disappointed: it was all so peaceful and rustic. We scrambled to the foot of the cliff and walked along a path, looking up at the rocks as we went. There was nearly a mile of them – all very steep, seamed with cracks, weathered by wind and rain, sometimes completely hidden by the trees or covered by an uninviting black slime, but where the trees had receded there were stretches of clean grey-brown rock. As we walked along the foot, Cliff sounded like a guide in a stately home showing off the prized possessions to his visitors.

'That's Dick's Diversion up there,' pointing to a seemingly holdless vertical wall. 'It's one of the hardest routes here; I've never done it.' I wondered how anyone could, except perhaps a human spider – and then a bit farther on, he said, 'There's Slim Finger Crack – you can see why it's called that.' I could. The wall was overhanging at the bottom, and the crack that split it seemed barely wide enough to take one's fingers. It was difficult to believe that practically every square foot of rock had been climbed and had then been mapped and recorded, given a name and a standard of difficulty.

People were beginning to climb; for the most part they looped their climbing rope round a tree at the top of the rocks, tied on to one end, while a friend pulled it in at the bottom, so that they could not possibly hurt themselves if they slipped. This precaution was particularly advisable since the sandstone holds were often frail and could easily break off. We stopped to watch one of the climbers perform; there was already a good audience gathered at the foot of the cliffs. The climb, called Long Layback, ran up a steep crack of about thirty-five feet. He started off in fine form, his feet pressing against the rock at the side of the crack, his body almost parallel to the ground, leaning back on his arms. But then as he got higher he began to tire; his body sagged back on to the rope, and then the audience came to life, several climbers shouting different directions all at the tops of their voices.

'Cock your right foot up on to the scrape by your shoulder and lay back on the little pock.'

While another yelled, 'That's no good, Jack, jam your left foot in the crack to your left and reach up for the jug* . . . come on, reach, man, reach . . . you're nearly there.'

Jack, panting hard, – 'Tight rope . . . tighter, for God's sake' – gasps and grunts, and forces his unwilling body an inch higher, and the man holding the rope heaves and pulls at the bottom. But it's no good, he slumps back on the rope. Yells and ironic cheers from the audience.

'Let me down,' groans Jack.

'Come on, Jack. Have another go. You were nearly there,' shout the supporters' club.

'I can't. I've no bloody strength left in my arms and the rope's cutting me in two. Come on, let me down for Christ's sake.'

But his tormentors are now enjoying themselves.

'Go on, Jack. Fight it. You'll never make a mountaineer if you give in that easily.'

At this stage Jack is hanging unashamedly on the rope, having lost all contact with the rock, and is lowered to the ground. The next man quickly takes his place and starts up the crack, but because he has done the route many times before, climbs it quickly and easily.

*Jug-handle, a large hand-hold.

At Harrison's Rocks climbing becomes almost a spectator sport. People living in the area go there for their Sunday afternoon walk with the dog, and some of the climbers themselves rarely leave the ground but prefer to drift from audience to audience, to watch their friends and to talk about climbing.

Cliff soon had me on the end of a rope and I had my first taste of climbing. When he had gone up the narrow little chimney he had chosen for my first climb, it had looked easy, almost effortless – he had seemed to coax his way up the rock, stepping and pulling with a controlled precision; but when I followed I started to fight it and soon exhausted myself to no real effect, for I could make no further upward progress and all my struggles seemed to jam me even more firmly in the crack.

'Try to relax, Chris, you can't hurt yourself, you'll only come on to the rope,' Cliff said quietly.

I began to think, to look around me, to try and find somewhere to put my feet, something to pull on, and suddenly it was no longer a struggle, but an absorbing exercise.

I reached the top of that first climb and we went on to more, sometimes using the rope and on the shorter routes doing without it. There were plenty of climbs I could not get up, plenty of times when I began to fight, only to end by hanging on the end of the rope, to be lowered to the ground. By the end of the day my fingers were like strips of limp rubber and opened out the moment I pulled up on them; every limb ached with weariness. But what a day! I felt a sympathy with the rock; I found that my body somehow slipped into balance naturally, without any conscious thought on my part. There was not much height to worry about, for the crag was only thirty feet, but what there was didn't worry me; if anything, I found it stimulating. I knew that I had found a pursuit that I loved, that my body and my temperament seemed designed for it, and that I was happy.

Up to that time I had found no complete release in physical expression. Although I enjoyed rugger, I was always aware of my limitations, an instinctive fear of the ball, the slowness of my reactions. Even in the gymnasium I was limited. I lacked the speed of reaction to control my limbs with quick precision and, perhaps as a result, I always experienced a quick jab of fear as I launched myself into a vault or a handspring. This acted as a kind of brake, and I therefore often landed badly or ended the exercise in an uncontrolled tangle of arms and legs. But even on that first visit to the rocks, I experienced none of these limitations; I was conscious only of feelings of confidence and intense enjoyment that I had never experienced before.

(from *I Chose to Climb*)

The Interview

Write your answers as though you were the author himself.

1. It seems that your enthusiasm was greater than your common sense when you attempted Snowdon. What advice would you give to young people who are going hill-walking or climbing for the first time?
2. You say you read every book on climbing you could lay your hands on. How did reading books help you to become better at climbing, which is a physical activity and only mastered by practice?
3. You often mention the clothing the climbers wore – darned sweaters, ex-army windproofs and battered anoraks. Why do climbers take such a pride in wearing old and worn-out gear?
4. Why did you feel superior to the people on the train who were going to the seaside for the day?
5. Cliff was obviously a good teacher. What did you find so helpful in the way he introduced you to climbing?
6. What would you say you learnt about climbing when you attempted the narrow little chimney?
7. Why do you think you were so confident when you were climbing, yet felt such fear when you were playing rugger and doing gymnastics? Most people would be scared of climbing.
8. Would you say that great mountaineers are born and not made – yourself included?

Language

1. 'Jargon' is the specialised vocabulary used in a particular subject and not always understood by an outsider. Can you quote some examples of climbing jargon from the conversation of the bearded man in the Capel Curig youth hostel and from the comments of the audience at Harrison's Rocks?

2. Give some examples of jargon from other activities, such as football, racing, hairdressing, fashion, electronics, the armed forces, the theatre and popular music.
3. The following quotation is taken from an introduction to an English textbook. Which words and phrases would you class as jargon?

   Intended for use with classes in the middle school range, notoriously an area in which teachers of language arts find difficulty in assembling and structuring material . . . the lesson options suggest ways in which pupils might be involved in activities within the imaginative continuum of the core text.
4. Write some typical expressions that might be shouted by spectators during one of the following sports: wrestling, soccer, athletics, racing, boxing.

Class Conversation

Chris Bonington had no aptitude for rugger or gymnastics but had an immediate and instinctive love of climbing. What activities – not merely sporting ones – have you taken to with real keenness and are, perhaps, rather good at?

What are you no good at? Is there any point in trying to do things you dislike and have no ability for? Does fear ever enter?

Have you ever taken any physical risks that might have injured you or endangered your life? If you have, describe what happened. Why did you do it?

Chris Bonington was self-conscious about his appearance as a boy and felt shy and tongue-tied in the company of strangers. What sort of person do you find it easy to speak to? When do you find conversation with another person difficult?

Think of the attitude of the spectators at Harrison's Rocks as they watched the climbers. How do you behave when you are watching a sporting event? Are you usually quiet, tense, full of concentration, wild with enthusiasm, loudly critical? On what does your reaction depend? Has anything dramatic or exciting ever happened when you have been part of a crowd watching a game?

Has anyone been youth hostelling? How did you like living with others and doing a job in the hostel? Did you meet any interesting people?

The right sort of clothing seems to be important to climbers. When do you find yourself wanting to wear the 'right' clothes to identify you with a certain group of people or to express your personality?

Your own writing

You may adapt the suggestions below and write about them in any way you wish.

1. Write a story about a man or a woman who has a special gift, talent, skill or genius. Show how this is developed and whether the end result is success or failure.
2. Is enough done in schools and in society to help young people follow their genuine interests? What could be done to develop the talents and skills of young enthusiasts?
3. Write a dialogue or a short play featuring characters who are all keen on the same hobby, sport or occupation. Bring out their enthusiasm and, perhaps, their desire to show themselves knowledgeable or clever.
4. A youth hostelling adventure.
5. Take up some of the following comments on sport today and express your own opinion:
   'The trouble today is that too many people watch and not enough take part. The spectators – especially the young ones – have more energy than they use and it spills over into violence and vandalism.'
   'I'd rather watch sport on telly any day than go and see it.'
   'Being good at a sport isn't just being good in a physical sense, like being strong or fast or clever with your feet. You've got to have qualities of character as well if you are to succeed – courage, determination and will-power, for instance.'
   'Sport is ruined by professionalism.'
   'The Olympic Games do nothing but harm to international relations.'

6. Write a story in which the following sentence occurs: 'We were very green and were quite unprepared for the dangers ahead.'

Tape-recording

Choose a person in school, either pupil or teacher, who has excelled at a particular sport and arrange to interview him or her. Prepare your own set of questions and use any of the following that are appropriate. Tape-record the interview and play it back to the class.

When were you first introduced to the sport?

Did you have any help or encouragement from your parents or members of your family?

Do you owe a lot to your teachers?

How much training do you do?

Can you describe some of the most exciting events you have taken part in?

Is there anything in your temperament or character which helps you to be good at this particular sport?

Have you had to give up many ordinary pleasures, like going out in the evenings and at week-ends, in order to devote more time to training and playing?

Have you ever thought of becoming professional?

What advice would you give to anyone who wants to be really good at a sport?

Are you a good all-rounder, or are you hopeless at some sports?

Which sportsmen do you admire?

Sea-Signs
George Tardios

From the cliff-top
I watch a sailboat
Like a whip of wind
A white fleck in a fingernail of blue.

I have a photograph:
I fish off shallow rocks
With a long bamboo.
Waves clash
Spray dots my picture.
In summer I am surrounded by flecks of snow.

Melon seeds and coca-cola cans
Black olives like goat droppings
Collect on the water.
The sea has spread a blue tablecloth
And is having its picnic.

My face is caught in the water.
A small fish wriggles in my eye.

I dive from a caique
And meet myself
On the sea's skin.

The sea closes my mouth

It likes quiet.
I am a guest under its roof.

The fisherman on his boat
Peers into the sea.
I smile, half-asleep
Looking up at him.
Slowly rising
My lips touch his cheek.

Underneath
My flippers brush the reef surface.
My eyes reach the reef's shelf
And fall out of my head.

My spear misses the inkfish.
Cut
My feet leak
A wake of red smoke.
From behind its black cloud
The inkfish skids closer.

Under the stained glass surface
Sunlight falls in shafts.
Spread-eagled in this cathedral
I fly over valleys
In spring bloom.

On the sea's marriage bed
Glowing fish thread themselves
Into veils of bright beads.
I kneel in pillows of sand
And they weave a groom's jewels around my head.

The sea has entered my blood
Its minerals live in my bones.
My tears are the salt sea in my eyes
My sweat is the salt sea on my skin.
On the sand's heat
Oceans break from me

I hear my fathers sing
Like Sirens.

Considering the poem

1. *Sea-Signs* is rich in figurative language. Go through the poem
   and quote what you consider to be effective and imaginative
   metaphors and similes.
2. Where do you detect a touch of humour in the poem?
3. Can you suggest what is actually happening when George Tardios writes:
   a) *Slowly rising*
      My lips touch his cheek.
   b) *My eyes reach the reef's shelf*
      And fall out of my head.
   c) *I fly over valleys*
      In spring bloom.
4. As Christian Bonington felt an instinctive attraction to mountains, so George Tardios feels an ancient and inborn love of the
   sea. Where is this feeling expressed in the poem?

Your own writing

Write in free verse or in prose on one of the following:

1. Choose a subject of physical movement which you yourself
   enjoy, such as swimming, running, dancing, cycling, gliding,
   playing a game or, like the poet, skin-diving. Describe an occasion when you take part in this activity, what stages you go
   through, what you see of your surroundings, what sensations
   you feel, and how your imagination responds to the experience.
   Write as though it is happening *now*.
2. Find some photographs of yourself as a child. Describe what
   you are doing in the photographs and the occasions on which
   they were taken.
3. Sun. Sea. Sand. Sails.

Doing a Bunk
Leslie Thomas

Leslie Thomas was an orphan and for part of his childhood he lived in Dr. Barnardo's Home ('Dickie's') in Kingston upon Thames. He had been separated from his younger brother, Roy, who was sent to live with foster-parents in Long Crendon, Buckinghamshire. Leslie has not seen his brother for eighteen months and, fearing that he might lose touch with him altogether, decides to run away from Barnardo's to find him. He takes with him half a tin of toffees – Roy's share of a present which had been sent by an elder brother.

I selected Sunday for the start of my journey to visit my brother, because it was the day we wore our suits and I thought it would be a good idea to go looking presentable. My suit was dark blue, and we had just been given a consignment of eggy yellow ties, and I had one so I thought I would wear that too. I also had my banana-coloured gloves, which I had bought in King's Lynn, and it did not occur to me that either they or the tie might make me conspicuous.

At breakfast I managed to pick up two boiled eggs instead of one, and an extra slice of bread. I had three apples and about two and eightpence. It was the money which was troubling me. I had been without dush for a couple of weeks for some misdemeanour and two shillings and the few pence was the most I could gather. By selling some of my prized personal possessions, at bargain prices and to hard buyers who knew I wanted the money desperately, I made some funds and I managed to borrow the odd penny or twopence at school.

My original plan was to bunk immediately after breakfast, but there was a chance that the Gaffer would miss me if I didn't go to church. Today might be the day that he decided to make a check. You could never tell with the Gaffer.

So we marched to church like we did every Sunday, with the Gaffer sniffing the air along the pavement while we stepped it out in the road, and all the people stared and said, 'Oooh, poor little chaps', so that you wanted to stick your tongue out at them.

Church was hollow and unholy as it always was. It was dreary, with none of the warmth of the church at Narborough, none of its comfortable, living feeling, none of its help to God. This church gave you the feeling that it was only opened on Sunday and then shut up thankfully for the rest of the week. It was a necessary evil, like Matron's Bible Class.

We used to sit in the balcony, so that we were out of the way and what was going on down below was remote. If you were far enough out of the Gaffer's eye you could read comics.

The odd thing was that the barber who used to chop off our hair would appear on the other side of the balcony, always halfway through the service, puffing and looking apologetic as though he had sinned deeply on his way there. Always the Gaffer would see him and, after privately noting the time of his arrival, would give him a quick churchy nod.

The barber was the only one who ever sat in the balcony apart from us, and sometimes I thought that perhaps he only came so that the Gaffer would see he was a church-going man and allow him to continue to cut our hair. On the other hand he may have really enjoyed his worshipping.

We returned to the regular Sunday lunch, a stone wall of jacketed potatoes piled on their trays, the expressionless cold meat and the moribund butter beans. Then the currant pudding and custard. And after that I was away. It was my plan to cut across Richmond Park and go from there to Ealing, which was the first of the towns on the map I had drawn of my route to Long Crendon. With me I had the retired music case in which I normally carried my school books, and inside it was the hard boiled egg, the bread, the apples, a pencil and paper, and my brother's toffees in their tin. The map I had in my pocket.

It was nearly October and the day had seen the passing of full rain clouds across the sky. As I walked over the grass of the park and under the trees, the big clouds were crowding together and it looked like rain. Lines of beech trees on the rising ground stood out like bones against the dark. Up and down the small hills and down again, so that I imagined it was the ribbed skeleton of a long and ancient animal lying there. The grass and heather of the park were worn out from the summer and they felt old and fragile under my shoes as I went. It was not a good day and I seemed to be alone there. No people, no animals and hardly a bird. It was quiet and still and waiting for the rain.

The rain came in round, marble drops, rattling in the trees, drumming among the grass and causing the heather to tremble. The clouds seemed to be climbing on each other's backs in their hurry and the splashes joined together into a downpour. Now, I thought, was the time to go back, really. I was under a tree and none of the rain was coming on me, but now was the time to make up my mind whether to go on or not. If I returned my steps now – or anyway after the rain had stopped – there was a good chance that I would not have been missed, and I would have dodged Matron's Bible Class, which was always a good thing.

A busy stream had appeared from somewhere inside the tree, and was running down the trunk and on to the ground at my feet. But the rain ceased quite quickly and I saw a man on a bicycle coming along the road from the far end of the park. He had a rigid overcoat pulled up around his head, and his neck hunched into the coat. He pedalled up the road and passed near me but he did not see me. I came from under the tree and went up to the road out of the wet grass.

Some of the sky was empty now, that distinct blue emptiness that comes after autumn or spring rain. But there were still corpulent black clouds, and one especially big with the sun shining at the back of it and the beams flung out as though God himself were behind it. I reached the road and turned towards Richmond because I had decided to go on. The journey to my brother lasted about five days. I walked a good part of the way, resting away from the road every so often in a field or a lane. Twice I got good long lifts, once on a lorry and once in a van, but the driver of the van misunderstood the place I wanted to go and I went miles astray.

He did not ask me where I had come from, nor did he seem to need to know anything else about me. He was a young man in blue overalls, and he whistled through his teeth all the time we were travel-

ling. Then when the lorry stopped the driver had a big bundle of a
dog in the cab. 'If you want a lift you'll have to get on the back,' he
said. Then he laughed and called after me: 'That's if you can stand
it.' I climbed on to the back of the lorry and I understood what he
meant. He had been around the countryside collecting swill for pigs.
There were six or seven bins full of it and it slopped and flopped over
the side as the road bent and the lorry jumped. The smell unfurled
behind the bins, fluttering like a banner, and although I crouched
right on the tailboard, with my head hanging over the side, I could
still not avoid it.

At nights, during the journey, I slept twice under bridges; once
under a railway bridge and once under a bridge across a river with a
small path where the arch and water touched. There was a leaf-
shaped boat pulled up on the path and a tarpaulin in the boat. I lay
in the boat, and it rained outside the bridge and the rain slipped off
the arch and into the river making a noise like a waterfall. Even
when the rain stopped I couldn't sleep because it dripped into the
river all night.

On the other two nights I slept in country bus shelters, on the
benches, with my collar pulled right up and my face turned away
from the road so that it would not show up white to anyone passing.

It was strange, for no one bothered me all the time I was on my
way. You might have thought that a boy in a deformed blue suit,
with a yellow tie, yellow gloves and a music case, might have
attracted some curiosity, but I did not. I made sure that I did not
look too vagabond by carefully washing in a stream or river as soon
as I could each day, combing my hair and trying to keep my shirt
and tie straight.

Before I had set out the thought that worried me most was that I
might get so hungry that I would have to give myself up. But on the
road I had no anxiety because there were orchards still bushelled
with fruit, and it lay clustered in the autumn grass under the
hedgerows. There were still blackberries in the thorns, and I col-
lected ears of wheat, left lying in open fields after the harvesting,
and munched it as I went.

In Wendover I bought a loaf of bread from a woman in a baker's
shop, who looked at me in a strange way, and I bought a couple of
buns the next day from another place.

It was a fine journey really. It did not rain very much in the day
and although I got tired I was never sad. I found that if you did not

think of the steps you were pacing, or count the miles too diligently, the places you aimed for seemed to arrive so quickly that they might have set out themselves to meet you half-way.

There was plenty to see and think about. There were grey and red houses sitting like resting travellers at the roadside and others by themselves up on the brows of the gentle Chilterns. I wondered why people should build houses like that, away and alone, with a valley and perhaps a wood between them and their neighbours. I would see a house like that, and imagine the man going gladly home in the evening and sitting out in front for a while and watching anything that was going on below. Or perhaps just sitting and watching nothing in particular but the light going off fields and the late sky and the dull shining of a river or stream.

Two of the afternoons turned warm and I got dusty and dry as I walked. My toes were uncomfortable too because my shoes were a bit small and my toes were always a funny collection anyway, all pushed and bunched together like people in a bus.

Autumn showed most in the trees. Where they stood together in woods or copses they were like girls standing together, each girl with a different colour hair.

Some of the fields were already turned and tilled, brown and vacant, with birds sitting on the furrows.

Sometimes, as I went, I would think about words. Not in any context or sentence, not in any poem or rhyme. But words for themselves alone, for what they were, simple and colourful and fine, each one a poem or a picture. Fall for autumn, sorrel for a horse, burnished for what the trees were. Just words. Lonely, loftily, topsail, reef, mist, oleander, isthmus, seascape, widgeon, conifer, quadrille, wild and wanderlust. Largo in music, sonnet in reading, Curaçao, Cayenne and Lourenço Marques for places that were far away.

As I walked towards Long Crendon, through the strange countryside and the unknown towns, I wondered how Roy would look now. It was a year and a half since I had stumbled from the ambulance with the woman promising that I would see him again the next day, and left him sitting up puzzled on the stretcher, with his small bundle of belongings on the floor.

It was in the late afternoon that I saw my first signpost with 'Long Crendon' on it. I was tired and there was a wind walking about in the trees; an autumn wind throwing birds and clouds about in the sky and singing a song of a cold night to come.

Long Crendon, said the signpost, was ten miles. Walking, weary as I now was, I knew I would never get there that night. It meant sleeping once more in some rough place, cold and aching and afraid again, listening for footsteps and watching for headlights on the road.

I walked for about half a mile up the road which went from the signpost. Then I stopped, and stood in the hedge for a while and watched a police car parked two hundred yards farther on. Presently a policeman appeared, turned the car around and drove off in the other direction. I went cautiously along through the briars and the ditches and came opposite the place where the car had been. It was a country police station, a house really, with a yard, a notice board, and a garage.

For a moment I had a suspicious, and thrilling, feeling that my picture might be on the notice board with the word 'Wanted' above it, and a full description, down to my yellow tie and my banana gloves, beneath. But there was no notice and nobody seemed to be about either, just the wind sweeping the yard and brushing the hedges and boughs.

At the moment when I was about to walk on, giving myself a mental warning to keep a watch for the police car returning, I noticed a shed at the side of the yard. Its roof slid low and it was open at the front. Inside were half a dozen bicycles.

It was a few strides across the yard. I took the bike that came first, which was also the oldest and most cranky, this being some saver for my conscience.

I ran with it across the yard and out into the road where I mounted it. It worked. It went. Apart from a tendency for the saddle to slip from side to side with each movement of the legs, it worked and went fine. Joyously now I rode, my music case hanging from the handlebars, the old bike going along like a charger suddenly freed from a stable. I knew the wind was with me for I could feel it pushing behind my ears, and pummelling my back, and the grey clouds raced along above me like a hunting pack. Once the music case slipped and fell on to the road, the tin of toffees inside it clanging as it hit the ground. The bike had no working brakes, I discovered at that moment, and I had to scrape along with my feet before I could stop it. Then, a few minutes later, a car rounded a curve far ahead and, thinking it was the homing police car, I swerved the bike recklessly from the road, collided with a gate and completed the spectacular movement by somersaulting from the saddle into the field.

The car went past without stopping and I was crouching in the hedge at that time, so I did not know whether it was the police car or not. I pushed off again, the way the clouds were running. The figures on the signposts diminished. At last there was one which said 'Long Crendon 1 mile.'

It was evening everywhere now, broken clouds over broken fields, with the trees becoming smudgy and merged, early lights in far windows and smoke curling like locks of dark hair. The road led straight into the village. I had never been there before and I never went there again, but I remember a big field with a low wall skirting it, and the road running along by the wall.

My brother was walking across the field, diagonally towards the road, as I pedalled along by the wall. Even though there was dusk and a year and a half between us, I knew it was Roy.

'Roy! Roy! Roy! Roy!' I don't know how many times I called, or why I kept calling like that, because he heard me first time and he knew it was me because he cried back and raced towards the gate in the wall.

He was running and I was pedalling, and I got there first, but the bike was going at such a pace that it slid beneath me and careered on as I jumped off. I fell over, then got up again, just as he was running to the gate.

He was not much different really, a bit taller, but skinny still, and grinning with his broken tooth at the front, and his hair straight down over his eyes. He climbed on the gate and dropped over.

We just stood, facing each other, neither of us knowing what to do next. My instinct was to put my arms around him because he was my brother and I loved him dearly, but boys don't do that sort of thing easily. And it seemed too formal, too grown up, to shake hands. That would have been just as foolish.

So I said: ' 'lo Roy.'

' 'ello Les,' he said.

'Here,' I said, fumbling in my music case. 'I've got some toffees for you.' Because they had not liked his name, his foster parents called him George. This made me angry at the time, and still does. It was not sufficient that he, at nine years of age, should suddenly be taken from everything he knew, but after going through the pipeline of the system he should find himself with a new name.

His foster parents were kind country people with a small house where they made me a bed on the landing. But to them he was George, and at school he was George. It reeked of injustice to me. Roy, after all, was good enough for his first mother.

I sat on the end of his bed for hours that night and we talked quietly like two mice. Talked of all the days we had known together, and the days since, and all that had happened. He had been the most unhappy after we had been parted, and he kept writing letters to our mother and getting no reply. When the Martin family went to see him and told him that she had been dead for a year he had cried, but felt relieved in an odd way too, because he had thought that she did not want to have anything to do with him any more. He was content now in this small place. It was strange to hear him call the woman in the house Mum, and to hear him say that his father was a thatcher. He talked of villages around the countryside, and boys at school, and summer cricket matches, and how they had been down to Marlow and the Thames for a holiday. All the things we had known, the lamp-post games on winter nights, the dusty street in August, the Ebbw coal we cut from the black river bank, our friends and foes, our parents and the big black and white cat, were all of a different time and a different place, and would never be ours again. But he was no stranger to me, nor I to him. For this I was happy and thankful. I had often wondered if he would still be my brother when I found him again. And he was.

On the following day I took the bike from the front door and returned the way I had come. Roy's foster parents did not ask me how I had made the journey, and I did not tell them, nor him.

Roy walked down to the wall and the gate with me. We knew that we would never lose each other again. He climbed on the wall and waved as I went away, and he was still waving as I turned the bend in the road and left the village behind.

Easily now I pedalled back to the police station, swerved into the yard spectacularly, and replaced the cycle in the litle shed with the others. I am certain that no one ever knew it was missing, certainly no one mentioned it to me.

I went to the door of the police station and gave myself up. A surprised-looking policeman with no helmet, and a cup of coffee in his hand, saw me standing there.

'I'm wanted by the police,' I said dramatically.

'Oh are you,' he said, taking a drink of coffee. 'Well it looks like we've found you don't it.'

Actually he'd never heard of me, which was a bit disappointing, but I had a fine lunch there, and a good tea in the afternoon, before they took me back to Dickie's in a police car.

I was apprehensive as the journey was getting towards its end. After all I had been away nearly a week and the Gaffer had been known to be tough about things like that. But at the door of Dickie's one of the staff matrons accepted me, and sent me upstairs for a bath. She said hardly anything at all and after I had bathed I was told to go to bed.

When the kids came up to the dormitory old Boz sat on the side of the bed and said: 'Did you 'ear about Cabbage-pants?'

'Did he bunk?' I said, slightly hurt that he hadn't asked me about my adventures.

'That's right,' he whispered. 'He did a bunk all right. Got on the railway line somehow last night, and a train came along and killed him. Joe Errington's just been up to see the body.'

(from *This Time Next Week*)

The Interview

Write your answers as though you were the author himself.

1. After all that, do you think it was worthwhile?
2. What sort of planning did you do before you ran away?
3. You must have felt very close to your brother to have wanted to make this difficult journey to see him. Why do you think there was such a strong feeling between you?
4. Did you ever consider that perhaps your brother had changed and that your meeting with him might prove a disappointment?
5. Would you say you were lucky in the people you met on the way?
6. What was the worst part of the journey? And the best?
7. What were your thoughts when you were being driven in the police car back to the orphanage?
8. You must have had a good tale to tell when you got back to Dickie's. What did you tell the boys?

Class Conversation

The relationship between Leslie and his brother was a close one and their affection for each other seemed as though it would last. What is your experience of relationships between brothers and sisters within a family? Are there quarrels? What are they usually about and how do they get sorted out? Are there times when you get on well together? What unites you?

Have you ever 'run away' from home or school or any other place? If you have, why did you do it? What did you want to get away from? What did you hope to gain by running away? How did you eventually return?

Have you ever been on a long journey – walking, cycling, by car, coach, train or aeroplane? Why did you undertake it? What incidents happened on the way?

What are the pleasures and discomforts of sleeping rough?

Leslie's encounter with the policeman was a short and pleasant one. It's not unusual for young people to become involved with the police over minor offences. Has anyone had a brush with the law?

Leslie felt that a grave injustice had been done by his not being allowed to see Roy and this prompted him to rebel, to leave Barnardo's without permission. What kinds of unfairness and injustice cause young people to rebel against authority? Have you sometimes felt you wanted to protest against an injustice? What did you do?

Language

1. The writing is simple, but there are some very imaginative passages that read almost like poetry. In describing Sunday lunch, for instance, the author writes:
   a *stone wall* of jacketed potatoes piled on their trays, the *expressionless* cold meat and the *moribund* butter beans . . .
   There are many colourful comparisons also:
   Lines of beech trees on the rising ground stood out *like bones against the dark*.
   Below are some quotations from the passage containing similar imaginative words, phrases and comparisons. Write out the quotations and underline the expressions which you consider to

be good examples of imaginative writing:
a) *the retired music case*
b) *The grass and heather of the park were worn out from the summer and they felt old and fragile under my shoes as I went.*
c) *The rain came in round, marble drops, rattling in the trees, drumming along the grass and causing the heather to tremble. The clouds seemed to be climbing on each other's backs in their hurry and the splashes joined together into a downpour.*

2. Can you find some more examples of colourful and imaginative writing from pages 51–59?
3. Leslie Thomas at that early age was interested in words *for themselves alone . . . simple and colourful and fine, each one a poem or a picture.* Read again the paragraph beginning *Fall for autumn . . .* , then make a list of words which you yourself like the sound of.

Sketches and role-play

1. Prepare and perform sketches based on:
   a) a person giving himself up at a police station;
   b) a meeting of two people who haven't seen each other for years;
   c) the interview between Leslie and the Gaffer on Leslie's return to the home;
   d) a hitch-hiker thumbing a lift and being picked up by a motorist or lorry driver;
   e) sleeping in a public place and being woken up in the morning rather suddenly.

2. Set up an inquiry into Leslie's running away to decide whether or not he should be punished. The class will ask the questions and come to a verdict. The witnesses will be the main characters in the story: Leslie, Roy, the Gaffer, the policeman, Roy's foster parents, another boy from Barnardo's – and anyone else who might usefully be called to give evidence about Leslie's character. Did he have criminal tendencies? He stole food and a bicycle. Was he justified in running away? Why hadn't he been allowed to see Roy before? Will the Gaffer lose his authority if he lets Leslie off? Why should a boy commit suicide? These are

some of the questions that might be asked. Use the information you are given about the characters in the passage and add some realistic touches of your own if you are playing one of the roles.

Your own writing

1. A conversation at night. Write about two people talking at night – perhaps recollecting the past, plotting something, arguing, dreaming about the future or simply going over the day's dramatic or amusing events. Set the scene first of all, then develop the conversation so that it reaches a conclusion or a climax.

2. 'I was determined to find him (or her)!' Describe your search for a 'lost' character.

3. A special journey. Bring into your writing some description of the nature of the country you were travelling through, how the weather affected you and what incidents occurred on the way.

4. 'But I didn't steal it – I just borrowed it!' Write a story in which one of the characters says this.

5. Young people and crime. Choose three or four aspects of this topic and write briefly about each one, or write a longer essay on one topic. You might consider some of these aspects: What are the most common crimes committed by young people today? Can you quote any typical examples? How serious are these 'crimes'? How important is family and upbringing? What influences are there on young people today which might lead them into crime? What punishments are given and what effect do they have? What misdemeanours are committed by young people that don't quite amount to crimes? What relationship exists between the police and teenagers? What can schools do to help pupils stay on the right side of the law?

Letter to Barbados
Ted Walker

Dear far-off brother, Thank you for yours,
And for the gift you send of little shells.
Evening. It has been an April day
Like any you remember. I guess
How you miss the English spring, the way
A shower-cloud over the hillside spills

Between sunlight and sunlight, slowly.
Is it half a year since you've been gone?
While you gather up windfall nutmegs,
My white magnolia flowers fly
Withering from the twig like cotton rags
I must rake tomorrow from the lawn.

I wonder what news you want to hear:
That everything remains as it was
Before you left? That we are well? That
Swallows, like molecules of summer,
Warm on the wall behind the dovecote?
All is satisfactory in this house.

I read over again what you tell me.
Outside your window you've had grapefruits
Ripening through the winter; there's a calf
You love to let suck your fingers. I
Relish these images of your new life,

Though the dinning sun above you hurts

My eyes as I gaze. Easier for you,
Perhaps, to think back to the shadow
Of this temperate, darkening garden,
Where I sit and look for my last few
Doves to come home. They will soon swoop down,
Just as you recall they always do,

From the roof; each full throat soon will soothe
Nightfall once more. This morning I made
A first cut of the grass since autumn.
It smelt sweet in the sun, in the swathe
Where I left it to dry. I fetched my gun
And sought out a sickly dove and killed

It clean, and let it warm where it fell.
Whether it is white, loosened feathers
I glimpse in the half-dusk or blossoms
Lifting with the wind I cannot tell,
But I am glad to have you share them.
There are words not used between brothers,

And you will understand if I send
No more than these, the shrivelling details
Of another lost and uneventful day.
The birds are folded now. I shall stand
A moment more in the dead grass we
Walked on. My palms close cold over shells.

Considering the poem

1. Would you say the dominant tone of the poem was conversational or poetic? Can you give two or three examples of both
   ordinary, everyday language and the language we normally
   associate with poetry?
2. Letters to friends and relatives usually contain comments on a
   variety of personal topics, but Ted Walker's letter is much more
   limited. In a sentence, can you sum up the subject of the letter?

3. Do you think this piece of writing succeeds as both a letter and a poem or as only one of these?
4. Consider some of the remarks made in the poem and the incident concerning the sick dove. What impression have you gained of Ted Walker himself?
5. At a glance the poem looks extremely regular, each verse containing six lines and almost every line consisting of nine or ten syllables, yet when reading it one is hardly aware of the poem's structure. How has the poet managed this effect?

Your own writing

Write a letter-poem to a friend or relative, using some of the poetic technique you have studied in Ted Walker's poem – the informal, conversational style, the run-on lines, the simple verse form. You might choose to write about a particular day in the year which is typical of spring, summer, autumn or winter, describing what you are doing, or have done, and what your surroundings look like. You could write on several topics, as you would if you were writing an ordinary letter, yet giving your writing a touch of poetic language and the compression that is typical of poetry. You should, also, make some reference to the person you are writing to and to the letter you yourself have received. But your letter-poem will be largely about yourself – what you are currently thinking, feeling, doing and experiencing.

The Last Chance
Janet Hitchman

Janet Hitchman was an orphan and spent her childhood in various foster homes and institutions under the care of the Ministry of Pensions, which used to be responsible for the welfare of orphans. At the age of thirteen, Janet – or Elsie, as she was then called – was sent to one of Dr. Barnardo's homes where at first she lived in a 'cottage' with twenty-four other children of all ages who were looked after by a house mother. Eventually Elsie was moved to Meadow High School, a small boarding school within the institution or 'village' which was run by two teachers, the elderly Miss Julian and her young assistant and adopted daughter, Miss Blandford, to whom Elsie had become deeply attached. The extract below from *The King of the Barbareens* shows Elsie's determination to assert herself in the face of authority.

I took my time getting back to school, for the French lessons were held in a disused building at the other end of the village, and was met by an infuriated Miss Blandford, whom I had unwittingly kept waiting to begin an English lesson.

'Five hundred lines!' adding threateningly, 'by tonight.'

As I had passed the Junior Oxford and Agnes hadn't, I was in a class by myself, ostensibly studying for the School Certificate. Most of the time I worked on my own and as one of the set books was *Jane Eyre* I counted out five hundred lines of foolscap paper, and proceeded to fill them with an extract from that novel. Seeing myself as the ill-treated, misunderstood Jane, I read on and on after the five hundred lines were written, and finished the book. At the end I announced that I had changed my name to 'Janet', for that was what Rochester called his Jane in his fondest moments. By steadfastly refusing to answer to anything else, Janet I became, and am still.

Although in many ways I welcomed my release from loving, the fact that I seemed to be so shallow and devoid of loyalty worried me, and I felt now and then obliged to sting myself into championing Miss Blandford's cause. Once, a new house matron had arrived and had captured some of her admirers.

'I thought you cared for me' – wearing the air of a tragedy queen, Miss Blandford met me on the stairs.

'I do,' I answered, out of old habit.

'Miss C. is bathing in *my* water,' she swept past me and down. (The bath water was always a bone of contention between staff and children.) Perhaps she was really angry; or perhaps she was giggling at my discomfiture. I failed to see how I could prevent the amazonian Miss C. from bathing if the inclination took her. Great events do not hang on great beginnings, but depend upon the 'want of a horseshoe nail'. My kingdom was lost on bath water, for the next time Miss C. wanted to bath I treated her with such insolence that she threatened to resign.

She was a very good house matron, quite the most efficient we had yet been blessed with. Miss Julian certainly did not want to lose her; and I had long been a nuisance. I could not be got rid of on the grounds of intelligence. Every term two or more girls were turned out through not being up to standard. The school had grown, and so great was the pressure on places that only the very best could be kept on, especially after normal school-leaving age. The wails and sobs of those unlucky ones, who now had to resign themselves to being 'service girls', had haunted my dreams, and not even my adoration of Miss Blandford had caused me to neglect my school work. I could, however, be removed as an 'upsetting influence'. My temper was still uncontrollable at times, and I had little respect for rules. I had often been warned that this state of affairs could not last, and since the summer I considered I had been very good. It had been easier to behave, now that I was growing out of adolescent 'pashes', and had I been left alone I should have developed quite normally.

In the summer I had defied the whole school and received a 'last and final' warning. It had been appallingly hot, and the crowded bedrooms were like furnaces. It must have been the summer of the yo-yo craze, for I was idly spinning one over the railings of the school steps, when we were ordered to bring our mattresses and blankets on to 'the back concrete'. The cottages were separated by fences and small asphalt yards; these yards in spite of their composition were always known as 'the back concrete'; and the path from the front door, which really was concrete, was called 'the front concrete'. Most of the girls thought sleeping out was a terrific idea, but I considered it a fag and not worth the effort. With bad grace I stuck my yo-yo in my garter; the securest place to keep anything of value. (The other garter kept safe a photograph of Miss Blandford, top half only. I had won it by force from another girl, who treasured her half – a pair of black stockinged legs.) I lugged my bedding outside, muttering about the daftness of sleeping next to the drains. Actually, I was frightened, not of anything in particular, but of all the things that could get at me much more easily outside than in. I crawled down underneath the blankets, covering myself completely; and I dreamt I was in front of a firing squad. There were others with me, and we were lined up with the tallest (me) at the back. The soldiers raised their rifles and shot the first one, who dropped, revealing the next, until it came to my turn. As the man was about to fire I woke up, and my first feeling was one of relief, 'I was about to die – and I *wasn't afraid.*' My next one was of panic, because although my eyes were open I could see nothing; also I had a violent pain in the middle of my back – the bullet obviously. Convinced now that the dream had been real, but that I was buried alive, I twisted and struggled in my grave of darkness; smelling what I was sure was the corruption of others who had died. I tore at the blackness above my head, and there, leering and mocking, hung the full moon, dragging up to herself the smell from the drains. The tightly wrapped blankets, the full moon, and, I discovered, the yo-yo on which I had been lying, had all combined to produce a nightmare; which had left me wet and jittering with fear. I had had enough; rolling up my bedding I went indoors, determined that no power on earth would get me camping out again. The next evening, which was just as hot, there was a scene because I refused to take out my bed. Afraid of Miss Blandford's mockery, I dare not give my reason, but resorted to being rude about the drains. If I had been able to explain to Miss Julian, no doubt she would have understood, for there was no reason why I should sleep outside, except that she had ordered it. With an omin-

ous, 'I'll deal with you in the morning', Miss Julian retired, and so
did I, praying 250 times 'Oh God let it rain'. I slept, to be awakened
about midnight by everyone rushing in out of a thunderstorm.
Murmuring 'Thank you, God', I rolled over to sleep again.

The next day Miss Julian gave me a solemn warning that I had
been given my last chance. 'One more outburst,' she promised, 'and
you shall go.'

After that for three months, until the bath water incident, I managed to keep out of trouble. Now with something like triumph Miss
Julian declared I had overstepped the mark; she would report me to
the Governor at once.

Another month went by, and I was hopeful that the matter had
been overlooked. I still went to school, and although no notice was
taken of me, I put it down to the need for concentration on the next
lot of school certificate candidates. Then I was called in to see a lady
from the Ministry of Pensions, Miss Hayes.

'I'm sorry to hear you are no longer happy at school,' she said.

'But I am.'

'I understand you have been giving trouble.'

'Not so much as all that.' This approach puzzled me.

'Have you decided what you want to be?'

'Of course, years ago. I'm going to be a librarian.'

'That needs training and a degree.'

'I shall get that all right. I'm taking the school certificate in July.'

It had all been so plain. School Certificate, college, a degree and
then librarianship.

Miss Hayes fumbled for her words.

'But I'm afraid you have spoiled all that. Barnardo's won't keep
you any longer, and *we* haven't any funds. Now it means a job.'

'You mean I have to leave school?'

'We have been asked to remove you.'

'But I can't leave school. I've *got* to be a librarian; there isn't
anything else I can be.'

'We must – think of something.'

I went out of the room as from a death sentence. Nothing, I felt,
could be more unjust. It had never occurred to me that this was what
Miss Julian had been threatening. I thought the worst that could
happen would be that I should be moved to another cottage. That I
should have to give up everything that I wanted, and have to leave
the village in shame like any laundry girl – this I had never thought
possible.

I went to see mother, who had moved next door and was in charge of the junior girls. She was sympathetic. In the old days she would have be-hatted herself and been across the green to the Governor. But now, since the changes had come, she seemed to have lost some of her old spirit. 'I miss the babies,' she had said once. Now she said, almost to herself:

'I knew no good would come of this school. They've run beyond themselves.'

'But I haven't been all that bad,' I sobbed. 'Gertrude is much worse than I am, but *she* keeps at school.'

'Why not go and apologize to Miss Julian? Perhaps things will be all right again, and you can live here with me.'

Cheered and comforted, pathetically certain that mother would make everything right, I knocked on Miss Julian's door, my apology beautifully poised in my mind. She eyed me over the tops of her spectacles, her small straight mouth almost invisible. Miss Blandford stood by the window.

Before I could speak Miss Julian began. 'We shall want your uniform for another girl, so collect it together. For the few days you will be here, you can wear play clothes.'

I did not speak a word, but went out already undoing the buttons of my tunic. I wanted to tear it to pieces, anything for action; anything to stop someone else wearing it. Miss Blandford followed me out.

'I'm sorry it's like this,' and as if she read my thoughts; 'don't do any damage to that uniform. There might be a chance, just a chance, you may need it again.'

'Why should I have to leave?' I burst out. 'Why me? What have I done that Gertrude hasn't done worse?'

'It isn't our fault. We pleaded, but the Ministry insisted you left.' This was a lie, as I was later to learn.

The Ministry, at a loss to know what to do with a half-trained girl, had wanted me to stay. It was they who pleaded; and Miss Julian who insisted. This lie was to colour my attitude to the Ministry for several years, until I learned the truth.

Another fortnight dragged by and Miss Hayes came again.

'It has been decided to give you another chance – but not here,' she added hastily. 'You are going to board with a lady; and will go to Clark's College, where you will study for a Civil Service examination.'

This didn't sound so bad, and I cheered up for a little while, until Miss Blandford sneered, 'Civil Service! A nice safe job with a pension! When you could have done – anything!'

Like a somnambulist I got through the days of outfitting. I was surprised to find that other people were not concerned with my failure; they seemed to think that I had done quite well. Miss Thomas went out of her way to give me the best clothes she had in the store; and, moreover, produced a suitcase to carry them in. Service girls had boxes, and boarders-out blue canvas sacks; but drowned in shame and selfish misery, I did not then appreciate her kindness.

The last day came; and I stood in my brand-new clothes, underneath which a full-size pair of corsets creaked like a suit of armour; restraining a concave stomach and two little knobs above. I had not cried until the moment of parting. Up till now, deep within me, I had believed that something, someone would save me.

'Don't forget,' whispered Miss Blandford diabolically. 'In about six months write to Miss MacNaughton and ask if you can come back.'

Bessie carried my suitcase for me to the Governor's House. My tears made me almost blind. Many eyes were on me as I went through the village, and there were loud comments on my clothes and suitcase. My tears were unremarked, for everyone cried when leaving the village, even if they had been miserable there.

The Governor, cold as at my reception, bade me a short farewell. I wanted to fling myself at her feet and beg to be allowed to stay, but this was real life, not the stage; I just dumbly joined the anonymous Ministry officer, and went through the main gates to the tram. Leaving behind me that small closed world, that had for three years held all my dreams, and shown me visions of life as it might be; even 'poor little, plain' as I was. Leaving the library and the cool picture gallery behind it – the cups marked 'Beta Cafe' and 'Royal Zoological Society'; the phrases 'Lick your spoon and keep it' after soup; 'Governor's notice – pass it on' – 'Look at the Meadow Muck School, Coo-er' – and the babies, babies, babies.

The tram conductor reversed the power arm; sending out bright blue electric flashes. The driver walked through the vehicle, turning the back into the front. We mounted the platform; a whistle shrieked, and we clattered towards the City.

(from *The King of the Barbareens*)

The Interview

Imagine that Janet Hitchman is being interviewed about this extract from her autobiography. Choose some of the following questions to put to her and write your answers as though you were the author herself.

1. Did you get much opposition to changing your name from Elsie to Janet? It must have been a difficult thing to do, especially in your situation.
2. You say you welcomed your *'release from loving'*. In what sense was it a 'release'?
3. Why did you behave so insultingly to Miss C. over the bath water? It seemed a minor incident, yet it ended with your being sent away from Barnardo's. Were you really free of Miss Blandford?
4. Do you think the adolescent 'pash' you had on Miss Blandford was a harmless and normal emotional stage to go through at your age?
5. You defied the whole school by refusing to sleep out on the concrete! You were very determined! Looking back, do you think you were right? What would happen to discipline if everybody pleased himself?
6. If you had been given a chance to speak during the interview with Miss Julian, what would you have said?
7. After the interview with Miss Hayes, when she told you that you had to leave Barnardo's, you felt that nothing could be more unjust. Why was your dismissal unjust? Hadn't you been a very difficult pupil – insolent and disobedient?
8. Why do you say that Miss Blandford whispered *diabolically* that you should write after six months and ask to come back?
9. What did you like about life at Barnardo's?

Class Conversation

My temper was still uncontrollable at times. Uncontrollable temper is not exactly uncommon! Think about 'tempers' at home, in school, in sport, whilst driving on the roads – to name but a few situations. What causes bad temper – your own in particular? Can you control it? Who can and who can't?

... and I had little respect for rules. Why should one respect rules? Which rules do you yourself break? Which rules do you consider necessary and useful?

Elsie disliked the idea of sleeping outside because, amongst other things, she was frightened of *all the things that could get at her.* How many of you have fears of animals and insects? Has anyone ever attempted to overcome his fear?

Writing out 'lines' is one of the oldest forms of punishment in our schools. Have you ever had to write out lines? What do you think of it as a punishment?

Elsie changed her name to Janet. Are you happy with your name – both forename and surname? Why should a woman adopt her husband's name when she marries? What's in a name?

It isn't often we can remember our dreams or nightmares. Can anyone? What causes them? Have they any significance?

Looking at details

1. Can you explain the reference to the *want of a horse-shoe nail*? (page 67, line 18). You may find it in a book of poetry or in a dictionary of quotations.
2. Read again the description of Janet's dream. It suggests that, though dreams are in the imagination, they have their basis in real events. What causes Janet to imagine: *a)* that she had been shot in the back; *b)* that she had been buried alive; *c)* that there was a smell of corruption?
3. Explain the meaning of the words in bold type in the following quotations from the passage:
   a) who I had **unwittingly** *kept waiting* (page 66, line 17)
   b) **ostensibly** *studying for the School Certificate* (page 66, line 21)
   c) The bath water was always **a bone of contention** *between staff and children* (page 67, line 14)
   d) the **amazonian** *Miss C.* (page 67, line 17)
   e) I was growing out of adolescent **'pashes'** (page 67, line 36)

f) *I* **lugged** *my bedding outside* (page 68, line 13)

g) *smelling what I was sure was the* **corruption** *of the others who had died* (page 68, line 27)

h) **leering** *and mocking, hung the full moon* (page 68, line 29)

i) *With an* **ominous,** *'I'll deal with you in the morning,'* (page 68, line 40)

j) *Like a* **somnambulist** (page 71, line 4)

k) *My tears were* **unremarked,** *for everyone cried when leaving the village* (page 71, line 22)

l) *I just dumbly joined the* **anonymous** *Ministry officer* (page 71, line 26)

Your own writing

1. Short plays or dialogues:
   a) Imagine that Janet had been able to begin her explanation when she went to see Miss Julian, as the cottage mother had suggested. Dramatize the interview, but choose a different ending if you wish.
   b) The discussion between Miss Julian, Miss MacNaughton (the Governor), Miss Hayes (the lady from the Ministry of Pensions) and Miss Blandford on whether or not to make Janet leave Barnardo's.
   c) Any situation in which a person is being dismissed or expelled.
   d) Some of the difficulties and frustrations of sleeping out of doors or camping.
2. Nightmare. You might describe the events that cause the nightmare, then the nightmare itself. Make it different: don't end with, 'then I woke up'.
3. A dramatic or humorous incident in the life of one of the following: a prisoner, a hospital patient, a fireman, a policeman, a visitor to a holiday camp, a welfare officer.
4. Imagine that you have left school for a few years. Write a letter to one of your old teachers, telling him or her how you are getting on and what you think of your schooldays, now that they are behind you.
5. Injustice!
6. Write on one or more of the topics discussed in 'Class Conversation'.

Warning
Jenny Joseph

When I am an old woman I shall wear purple
With a red hat that doesn't go, and doesn't suit me,
And I shall spend my pension on brandy and summer gloves
And satin sandals, and say we've no money for butter.
I shall sit down on the pavement when I'm tired
And gobble up samples in shops and press alarm bells
And run my stick along public railings
And make up for the sobriety of my youth.
I shall go out in my slippers in the rain
And pick the flowers in other people's gardens
And learn to spit.

You can wear terrible shirts and grow more fat
And eat three pounds of sausage at a go
Or only bread and pickle for a week
And hoard pens and pencils and beermats and things in boxes.

But now we must have clothes that keep us dry
And pay the rent and not swear in the street
And set a good example for the children.
We must have friends to dinner and read the papers.

But maybe I ought to practise a little now?
So people who know me are not too shocked and surprised
When suddenly I am old and start to wear purple.

Considering the poem

1. How old would you say the writer of the poem was?
2. Who do you think she is referring to in the second verse when she writes: *You can wear terrible shirts* . . . ?
3. What do we learn from the poem of the writer's attitude to dress, food, behaviour in public and spending money?
4. Which word, occurring at the beginning of most of the lines, creates the sense of breathlessness in the poem?

There aren't many of us who don't feel annoyed by petty restrictions and rules of conduct, whether they come from parents or teachers; and most of us, like Jenny Joseph, long to throw them off and please ourselves. What exactly are these restrictions and how would you behave if they were removed from you? What do you resolve to do in the future when you are your own boss and can do what you like? Write your own poem of rebellion or of your determination (if you have it – you may be perfectly happy as you are!) to do what you are prevented from doing now.

Seeing an Angel
Richard Wright

Richard Wright was born on a plantation in Mississippi in 1908 and in *Black Boy* he describes the suffering, poverty and racial prejudice which he experienced during his childhood and youth in the Deep South. The following extract, however, is concerned with a different kind of problem that faced him – the question of religious belief.

A religious revival was announced and Granny felt that it was her last chance to bring me to God before I entered the precincts of sin at the public school, for I had already given loud and final notice that I would no longer attend the church school. There was a discernible lessening in Aunt Addie's hostility; perhaps she had come to the conclusion that my lost soul was more valuable than petty pride. Even my mother's attitude was: 'Richard, you ought to know God through *some* church.'

The entire family became kind and forgiving, but I knew the motives that prompted their change and it drove me an even greater emotional distance from them. Some of my classmates – who had, on the advice of their parents, avoided me – now came to visit and I could tell in a split second that they had been instructed in what to say. One boy, who lived across the street, called on me one afternoon and his self-consciousness betrayed him; he spoke so naively and clumsily that I could see the bare bones of his holy plot and hear the creaking of the machinery of Granny's manoeuvring.

'Richard, do you know we are all worried about you?' he asked.

'Worried about me? Who's worried about me?' I asked in feigned surprise.

'All of us,' he said, his eyes avoiding mine.

'Why?' I asked.

'You're not saved,' he said sadly.

'I'm all right,' I said, laughing.

'Don't laugh, Richard. It's serious,' he said.

'But I tell you that I'm all right.'

'Say, Richard, I'd like to be a good friend of yours.'

'I thought we were friends already,' I said.

'I mean true brothers in Christ,' he said.

'We know each other,' I said in a soft voice tinged with irony.

'But not in Christ,' he said.

'Friendship is friendship with me.'

'But don't you want to save your soul?'

'I simply can't feel religion,' I told him in lieu of telling him that I did not think I had the kind of soul he thought I had.

'Have you really tried to feel God?' he asked.

'No. But I know I can't feel anything like that.'

'You simply can't let the question rest there, Richard.'

'Why should I let it rest?'

'Don't mock God,' he said.

'I'll never feel God, I tell you. It's no use.'

'Would you let the fate of your soul hang upon pride and vanity?'

'I don't think I have any pride in matters like this.'

'Richard, think of Christ's dying for you, shedding His blood, His precious blood on the cross.'

'Other people have shed blood,' I ventured.

'But it's not the same. You don't understand.'

'I don't think I ever will.'

'Oh, Richard, brother, you are lost in the darkness of the world. You must let the church help you.'

'I tell you, I'm all right.'

'Come into the house and let me pray for you.'

'I don't want to hurt your feelings . . .'

'You can't. I'm talking for God.'

'I don't want to hurt God's feelings either,' I said, the words slipping irreverently from my lips before I was aware of their full meaning.

He was shocked. He wiped tears from his eyes. I was sorry.

'Don't say that. God may never forgive you,' he whispered.

It would have been impossible for me to have told him how I felt about religion. I had not settled in my mind whether I believed in God or not; His existence or non-existence never worried me. I reasoned that if there did exist an all-wise all-powerful God who knew the beginning and the end, who meted out justice to all, who controlled the destiny of man, this God would surely know that I doubted His existence and He would laugh at my foolish denial of Him. And if there was no God at all, then why all the commotion? I could not imagine God pausing in His guidance of unimaginably vast worlds to bother with me.

Embedded in me was a notion of the suffering in life, but none of it seemed like the consequences of original sin to me; I simply could not feel weak and lost in a cosmic manner. Before I had been made to go to church, I had given God's existence a sort of tacit assent, but after having seen His creatures serve Him at first hand, I had had my doubts. My faith, such as it was, was welded to the common realities of life, anchored in the sensations of my body and in what my mind could grasp, and nothing could ever shake this faith, and surely not my fear of an invisible power.

'I'm not afraid of things like that,' I told the boy.

'Aren't you afraid of God?' he asked.

'No. Why should I be? I've done nothing to Him.'

'He's a jealous God,' he warned me.

'I hope that He's a kind God,' I told him.

'If *you* are kind to Him, He is a kind God', the boy said. 'But God will not look at you if you don't look at Him.'

During our talk I made a hypothetical statement that summed up my attitude towards God and the suffering in the world, a statement that stemmed from my knowledge of life as I had lived, seen, felt and suffered it in terms of dread, fear, hunger, terror and loneliness.

'If laying down my life could stop the suffering in the world, I'd do it. But I don't believe anything can stop it,' I told him.

He heard me but he did not speak. I wanted to say more to him, but I knew that it would have been useless. Though older than I, he had neither known nor felt anything of life for himself; he had been carefully reared by his mother and father and he had always been told what to feel.

'Don't be angry,' I told him.

Frightened and baffled, he left me. I felt sorry for him.

Immediately following the boy's visit, Granny began her phase of
the campaign. The boy had no doubt conveyed to her my words of
blasphemy, for she talked with me for hours, warning me that I
would burn forever in the lake of fire. As the day of the revival grew
near, the pressure upon me intensified. I would go into the dining
room upon some petty errand and find Granny kneeling, her head
resting on a chair, uttering my name in a tensely whispered prayer.
God was suddenly everywhere in the home, even in Aunt Addie's
scowling and brooding face. It began to weigh upon me. I longed for
the time when I could leave. They begged me so continuously to
come to God that it was impossible for me to ignore them without
wounding them. Desperately I tried to think of some way to say no
without making them hate me. I was determined to leave home
before I would surrender.

Then I blundered and wounded Granny's soul. It was not my
intention to hurt or humiliate her; the irony of it was that the plan I
conceived had as its purpose the salving of Granny's frustrated feelings towards me. Instead, it brought her the greatest shame and
humiliation of her entire religious life.

One evening during a sermon I heard the elder – I took my eyes off
his wife long enough to listen, even though she slumbered in my
senses all the while – describe how Jacob had seen an angel.
Immediately I felt that I had found a way to tell Granny that I
needed proof before I could believe, that I could not commit myself to
something I could not feel or see. I would tell her that if I were to see
an angel I would accept that as infallible evidence that there was a
God and would serve Him unhesitatingly; she would surely understand an attitude of that sort. What gave me courage to voice this
argument was that conviction that I would never see an angel; if I
had ever seen one, I had enough common sense to have gone to see a
doctor at once. With my bright idea bubbling in my mind, wishing to
allay Granny's fears for my soul, wanting to make her know that my
heart was not all black and wrong, that I was actually giving serious
thought to her passionate feelings, I leaned to her and whispered:

'You see, Granny, if I ever saw an angel like Jacob did, then I'd
believe.'

Granny stiffened and stared at me in amazement; then a glad
smile lit up her wrinkled white face and she nodded and gently
patted my hand. That ought to hold her for a while, I thought.
During the sermon Granny looked at me several times and smiled.

Yes, she knows now that I'm not dismissing her pleas from my mind. . . . Feeling that my plan was working, I resumed my worship of the elder's wife with a cleansed conscience, wondering what it would be like to kiss her, longing to feel some of the sensuous emotions of which my reading had made me conscious. The service ended and Granny rushed to the front of the church and began talking excitedly to the elder; I saw the elder looking at me in surprise. Oh, goddamn, she's telling him! I thought with anger. But I had not guessed one-thousandth of it.

The elder hurried towards me. Automatically I rose. He extended his hand and I shook it.

'Your grandmother told me,' he said in awed tones.

I was speechless with anger.

'She says that you have seen an angel.' The words literally poured out of his mouth.

I was so overwhelmed that I gritted my teeth. Finally I could speak and I grabbed his arm.

'No . . . N-nooo, sir! No, sir!' I stammered. 'I didn't say that. She misunderstood me.'

The last thing on earth I wanted was a mess like this. The elder blinked his eyes in bewilderment.

'What did you tell her?' he asked.

'I told her that if I ever saw an angel, then I would believe,' I said, feeling foolish, ashamed, hating and pitying my believing granny. The elder's face became bleak and stricken. He was stunned with disappointment.

'You . . . you didn't see an angel?' he asked.

'No, *sir!*' I said emphatically, shaking my head vigorously so that there could be no possible further misunderstanding.

'I see,' he breathed in a sigh.

His eyes looked longingly into a corner of the church.

'With God, you know, anything is possible,' he hinted hopefully.

'But I didn't see *anything*,' I said. 'I'm sorry about this.'

'If you pray, then God will come to you,' he said.

The church grew suddenly hot. I wanted to bolt out of it and never see it again. But the elder took hold of my arm and would not let me move.

'Elder, this is all a mistake. I didn't want anything like this to happen,' I said.

'Listen, I'm older than you are, Richard,' he said. 'I think that you

have in your heart the gift of God.' I must have looked dubious, for
he said: 'Really, I do.'

'Elder, please don't say anything to anybody about this,' I begged.
Again his face lit with vague hope.

'Perhaps you don't want to tell me because you are bashful?' he
suggested. 'Look, this is serious. If you saw an angel, then tell me.'

I could not deny it verbally any more; I could only shake my head
at him. In the face of his hope, words seemed useless.

'Promise me you'll pray. If you pray, then God will answer,' he
said.

I turned my head away, ashamed for him, feeling that I had
unwittingly committed an obscene act in rousing his hopes so wildly
high, feeling sorry for his having such hopes. I wanted to get out of
his presence. He finally let me go, whispering: 'I want to talk to you
sometime.'

The church members were staring at me. My fists doubled.
Granny's wide and innocent smile was shining on me and I was
filled with dismay. That she could make such a mistake meant that
she lived in a daily atmosphere that urged her to expect something
like this to happen. She had told the other members and everybody
knew it, including the elder's wife! There they stood, the church
members, with joyous astonishment written on their faces, whispering among themselves. Perhaps at that moment I could have
mounted the pulpit and led them all; perhaps that was to be my
greatest moment of triumph!

Granny rushed to me and hugged me violently, weeping tears of
joy. Then I babbled, speaking with emotional reproof, censuring her
for having misunderstood me; I must have spoken more loudly and
harshly than was called for – the others had now gathered about me
and Granny – for Granny drew away from me abruptly and went to
a far corner of the church and stared at me with a cold, set face. I
was crushed. I went to her and tried to tell her how it had happened.

'You shouldn't have spoken to me,' she said in a breaking voice
that revealed the depths of her disillusionment.

On our way home she would not utter a single word. I walked
anxiously beside her, looking at her tired old white face, the wrink-
les that lined her neck, the deep, waiting black eyes, and the frail
body, and I knew more than she thought I knew about the meaning
of religion, the hunger of the human heart for that which is not and
can never be, the thirst of the human spirit to conquer and transcend the implacable limitations of human life.   (from *Black Boy*)

The Interview

Write as though you were the author answering the questions in an interview.

1. What did you dislike most about the boy's attitude towards you?
2. You say it would have been impossible to tell the boy how you felt about religion; but if you had attempted it, what would you have told him?
3. You say that the boy had been carefully reared by his parents and had always been told what to feel. What's wrong with that? Shouldn't parents tell their children what to feel?
4. You say that you could not imagine God pausing in his guidance of the universe to bother about you. What do you think a believer would answer to that?
5. Who are you referring to when you say *after having seen His creatures serve Him at first hand, I had had my doubts*?
6. Do you think your Granny was wrong to try to get you to 'come to God?' And why was she so keen to do it?
7. You say you knew more than Granny thought you knew about the meaning of religion. What exactly is this 'hunger' and 'thirst' you speak of?
8. Granny comes out of the passage as a rather sad, pitiful old woman. Did you have any sympathy for her, even though you couldn't accept her views on religion?

Class Conversation

Read over the questions and choose one or two on which you can contribute to the class discussion.

Here we have two different viewpoints: the boy who believed and Richard who did not believe. Which viewpoint do you support?

Ought Richard to have allowed his Granny to believe that he had seen an angel – just to please her?

Religion was obviously very strong in Richard's family, yet he himself rejected it. Isn't the reverse usually true – that children tend to follow the religion of their parents?

What was your first acquaintance with religion? What were you taught to believe as a child? What views do you hold now?

Richard said his faith was anchored in what his mind could grasp or what could be explained rationally. What examples are there of belief in what cannot be proved? What cannot man explain?

In the passage there was a determined effort to persuade Richard against his will. In matters of religion are you subject to any persuasion or compulsion? Or are you allowed to please yourself?

What is there to be said for and against the following?
Religious assemblies in schools; the teaching of religious knowledge in schools; church-going; prayer; learning about other religions.

Sketches

Choose contrasting characters and perform sketches in which one person is trying to persuade another person to:

vote for a certain political party in an election;
believe in ghosts;
believe that UFOs are a reality;
lend him a pound;
sponsor him on a charity walk;
act in the school play;
agree with him on any controversial subject.

Word-study

Below are some quotations from the passage. Find the meaning of the words in bold type and answer the questions related to them.

1. *at* **public school** (in the American sense) (page 77, line 9)
   What would we call the same type of school in this country?
   What is an English public school?
2. *a* **discernible** *lessening in Aunt Addie's hostility* (page 77, line 10)
   What prefix would be added to make the opposite of *discernible*?
3. *in* **lieu** *of telling him* (page 78, line 15)
   What connection is there with *lieutenant*?

4. *words slipping* **irreverently** *from my lips* (page 78, line 36)
   What other words can you find that contain the idea of *to revere?*
5. *the* **destiny** *of man* (page 79, line 6)
   What common word comes from the same root?
6. *the* **consequence** *of original sin* (page 79, line 12)
   Find the meaning of these associated words: *sequel, sequence, inconsequent.*
7. *in a* **cosmic** *manner* (page 79, line 13)
   What is the connection between *cosmos* and *cosmetic?*
8. **tacit** *assent* (page 79, line 14)
   How does the word link up with the meaning of *taciturn?*
9. *a* **hypothetical** *statement* (page 79, line 27)
   What is the equivalent noun?
10. *the* **salving** *of Granny's frustrated feelings* (page 80, line 17)
    Find the meaning of the following words and show how they are connected: *salve, salvable, salver, salvia.*
11. **infallible** *evidence* (page 80, line 26)
    What is the opposite of *infallible?*
12. *I wanted* **to bolt** *out of it* (page 81, line 35)
    What other meanings can you find for *to bolt?*
13. *I must have looked* **dubious** (page 82, line 1)
    Look up *indubitable.*
14. **censuring** *her for having misunderstood* (page 82, line 27)
    What is a *motion of censure?*
15. **conquer** *and* **transcend** *the* **implacable** *limitations of human life* (page 82, line 40)
    What other words contain the idea of *trans,* meaning *to go across, through* or *beyond?*
    Find the meaning of: *to placate, placid.*

Your own writing

1. Choose one of the topics in 'Class Conversation' or 'Sketches' as the subject for an essay or a short story.
2. Imagine that you are writing to a friend who lives on the other side of the earth and who has very little knowledge of English life and customs.
   Select some examples to illustrate to your friend what happens during a typical English Sunday.

F

3. Describe and give your opinion of some of the television programmes that are concerned with religion.
4. The suffering in the world.
5. Three generations: what contrasts have you found in the lives and outlook of your grandparents, your parents and your own generation in the family?
6. Write a conversation between two people on the subject of religious or political belief. They need not necessarily disagree with each other.

FOR THEM
Stanley Cook

Righteousness is picked to the bone.

NO WAY. NO ENTRY. NO THROUGH ROAD.
NO ADMITTANCE EXCEPT ON BUSINESS.
NO HAWKERS. NO CIRCULARS. BEWARE OF THE DOG.

PASSENGERS ARE NOT ALLOWED TO RIDE ON THE PLAT-
    FORM.
Prickles about the bell push at the back.
PASSENGERS ARE NOT ALLOWED TO GIVE THE STARTING
    SIGNAL.
Halfway down the lower deck
A light on either side cocks a snook
In the safety of thick glass blisters.
SMOKING PROHIBITED. SPITTING PROHIBITED.

NO CASUAL CUSTOMERS. NO COACHES SERVED.
CLOSED EVEN FOR THE SALE OF WOODBINES.
DO NOT ASK FOR CREDIT: A REFUSAL OFTEN OFFENDS.
NO SMOKING. NO DOGS. NO PRAMS.

NO COLLECTION ON CHRISTMAS DAY AND BOXING DAY.
EMPTY. POSITION CLOSED. RETURNED TO SENDER.

NO CHILDREN. NO COLOUREDS OR CHILDREN.
NO CHILDREN, SORRY. BUSINESS LADY PREFERRED.

NO MID-DAY MEAL. NO VACANCIES.

PRIVATE. KEEP OUT.
THE PUBLIC ARE NOT ALLOWED TO CROSS THE LINE AT
    THIS POINT.
TRESPASSERS WILL BE PROSECUTED. BY ORDER.

NO UNAUTHORISED PERSON MAY OPERATE THIS HOIST.
PENALTY FOR IMPROPER USE £5.
NO SMOKING.

NO PARKING. PRIVATE PARKING. NO PARKING PLEASE.
CUSTOMER'S PARKING. NO PARKING EXCEPT FOR CORPO-
    RATION EMPLOYEES.
NO PARKING ON THESE GRASS VERGES.
NO WAITING THIS SIDE ON EVEN DATES.
DO NOT OBSTRUCT GARAGE ENTRY OPPOSITE.
IT IS DANGEROUS TO PARK ON THIS GANTRY.
NO LEFT TURN. ROAD CLOSED.

Cherub-shaped illuminations
Set a good example
By gazing at some prohibitions:
During the hours of darkness the iron rods
Supporting them remain invisible.

Stop picking at me.

Considering the poem

1. Why do you think most of the poem is written in capital letters?
2. Who is THEM in the title referring to?
3. Where would you expect to find the prohibitions quoted in each verse?
4. Why do the lights in the bus seem to have the courage to 'cock a snook' at the notices?
5. What does Stanley Cook mean by ending his poem: *stop picking at me*?
6. Can you say in one or two sentences what the basic idea of the poem is?

For you

We are all acquainted with most of the prohibitions quoted in the poem. There are many more, of course, and we come across them wherever we go. Think about some of the places where we might find them: in schools, at football matches, in clubs, in shops, at airports, on the roads, in hotels and boarding houses, in the countryside, in libraries, on trains. Do some 'field work' by going out and collecting examples yourself, then arrange them according to subject. Add some comments of your own in order to express an idea or a point of view about the prohibitions you quote. Write your own poem FOR THEM.

Instead of prohibitions, however, you could use the same idea and compose a poem based on one of these suggestions:
    advertising slogans and catch-phrases;
    slogans on badges and T-shirts;
    selected graffiti.

The Little Man
Hermann Hesse

Hermann Hesse was born in Calw, Germany, in 1877 and from his childhood onwards was something of a rebel. He resisted the traditional academic education and worked as a bookseller, an antique dealer and a mechanic. His first novel was published in 1904 and he went on to write masterpieces like *Siddhartha* and *The Glass Bead Game*. He won the Nobel Prize for Literature in 1946. The following passage is taken from an autobiographical essay published in 1923. Hermann Hesse died in Switzerland in 1962 where he had lived in self-imposed exile from his native Germany since 1919.

But of all the magic apparitions, the most important and splendid was 'the little man'. I do not know when I saw him for the first time, I think he was always there, that he came into the world with me. The little man was a tiny, grey, shadowy being, a spirit or goblin, angel or demon, who at times walked in front of me in my dreams as well as during my waking hours, and whom I had to obey, more than my father, more than my mother, more than reason, yes, often more than fear. If the little one were visible, he alone existed, and where he went and what he did I had to imitate. He showed himself in times of danger. If a bad dog or an angry bigger boy was plaguing me and my situation became critical, then at the most dangerous moment the little man would appear, running before me, showing me the way and bringing rescue. He would show me the loose board in the garden fence through which in the nick of time I could escape, or he would demonstrate for me just what I was to do – drop to the ground, turn back, run away, shout, be silent. He would take out of my hand something I was about to eat, he would lead me to the place where I could recover lost possessions. There were times when I saw him every day, there were times when he remained absent. Those times were not good, then everything was tepid and confused, nothing happened, nothing went forward.

Once the little man was running in front of me in the market square and I after him, and he ran to the huge fountain with its more than man-high stone basin into which four jets of water fell, he wriggled up the stone wall to the edge and I after him, and when from there he sprang with a vigorous leap into the water, I sprang too, there was no choice – and I came within a hairsbreadth of drowning. However, I did not drown, but was pulled out by a pretty young woman, a neighbour of ours whom I had barely known up to then and with whom for a long time I had a happy, teasing sort of friendship.

Once my father had to lecture me for a misdeed. I halfway exonerated myself, suffering once more from the fact that it was so hard to make oneself understood by grown-ups. There were a few tears and a mild punishment and in the end my father gave me, so that I should not forget the occasion, a pretty little pocket calendar. Somewhat ashamed and dissatisfied with the whole affair, I went away and was walking across the river bridge, when suddenly the little man ran right in front of me. Springing onto the bridge railing, he ordered me with gestures to throw my father's gift into the river. I did so at once; doubt and hesitation did not exist when the little man was there, they existed only when he was not there, when he had disappeared and left me abandoned. I remember one day when I was out walking with my parents and the little man appeared. He walked on the left side of the street and I followed him, and whenever my father ordered me back to the other side the little man refused to come with me and insisted on walking on the left side, and every time I had to go across to him again. My father got tired of the business and finally let me walk where I liked. He was offended and later, at home, asked me why I had been persistently disobedient and had insisted on walking on the other side of the street. At such times I was in serious embarrassment, indeed in real distress, for nothing was more impossible than to say a word about the little man to anyone at all. Nothing would have been worse, viler, more of a deadly sin than to betray the little man, to name him, to breathe a word about him.

I could not even think of him, not even call on him or wish him by my side. If he was there, it was good and I followed him. If he was not there, it was as if he had never existed. The little man had no name. The most impossible thing in the world, however, would have been, once the little man was there, not to follow him. Where he went, I went after him, even into the water, even into the fire. It was not as though he ordered or advised me to do this or that. Not to imitate something he did was just impossible as it would have been for my shadow in the sun not to follow my actions. Perhaps I was only the shadow or the mirror image of the little one, or he of me; perhaps when I thought I was imitating him I was acting before him or simultaneously with him. Only he was not, alas, always there, and when he was absent, then my actions lost all naturalness and necessity, then everything could be otherwise, then for every step there was the possibility of acting or not acting, of hesitation, of reflection. But the good, happy, lucky steps in my life at that time all occurred without reflection. The realm of freedom is also the realm of illusion, perhaps.

What good friends I became with the merry woman from next door who had pulled me out of the fountain! She was lively, young, pretty and dumb with an amiable dumbness that bordered on genius. She let me tell her stories about robbers and magicians, believing sometimes too much, sometimes too little, and considered me at least one of the wise men from the East, something I readily agreed to. She admired me greatly. If I told her something funny, she laughed loudly and immoderately long before she understood the point. I chided her for this, saying: 'Listen, Frau Anna, how can you laugh at a joke if you haven't understood it at all? That's very stupid, and besides it's insulting to me. Either you get my jokes and laugh, or you don't – then you shouldn't laugh and act as though you understood.' She went on laughing. 'No,' she cried. 'You are the cleverest youngster I've ever seen. You're great. You will be a professor or an ambassador or a doctor. But laughing, you know, is nothing to take amiss. I laugh just because I enjoy you and because you're the wittiest one there is. And now go ahead and explain your joke to me.' I explained it circumstantially, she still had to ask this and that, finally she really understood it, and if she had laughed heartily and generously before, now she really laughed for the first time, laughed quite madly and contagiously, so that I was forced to laugh too!

There were difficult tongue-twisters that I sometimes had to repeat to her, very fast, three times in a row. For example: 'Weiner Wascher waschen weisse Wasche'. (Viennese laundrymen wash white linens). Or the story of Kottbuser Postkutschkasten. She had to try them too, I insisted on that, but she started laughing first and could not bring out three words right, nor did she want to, and each sentence that she began ended in renewed roars of laughter. Frau Anna was the most joyous person I have ever known. In my boyish cleverness I considered her incredibly dumb, and actually she was, but she was a happy human being, and I am sometimes inclined to consider happy human beings the secret wise men, even if they seem stupid. What is stupider and makes people more unhappy than cleverness!

Years passed and my friendship with Frau Anna had fallen into abeyance. I was already an older schoolboy and subject to the temptations, sorrows and dangers of cleverness when one day I encountered her again. And once more it was the little man who led me to her. For some time I had been desperately struggling with the question of the difference between the sexes and the origin of children. The question became more and more burning and tormenting and one day it tormented and burned me so much that I would have preferred not to go on living unless this terrifying riddle was solved. Angry and sullen, I was returning from school across the market square, my eyes on the ground, unhappy and morose, and there suddenly was the little man! He had become a rare guest. For a long time he had been untrue to me, or I to him – and now I suddenly saw him again, small and nimble, running along the ground in front of me. He was visible for only an instant and then dashed into Frau Anna's house. He had disappeared, but already I had followed him into the house and already I knew why, and why Frau Anna screamed as I burst unannounced into her room, for she was just in the act of undressing, but she did not send me away, and soon I knew almost everything that was so painfully necessary for me to know at that time.

(from *Childhood of the Magician*)

The Interview

Answer the questions as though you were the author himself, using the information in the passage and what you can infer from it.

1. You say that the little man had no name – that it would have been a sin to name him. That, presumably, was when you were young. Can you give him a name now, or try to define him?

2. What do you mean when you say that the little man was an angel or a demon?

3. You say that it was impossible not to follow the little man and that you had to obey him *more than reason.* In which of the incidents do you think the little man was being 'unreasonable' – and it would have been better to disobey him?

4. Do you think there is a little man in everybody?

5. You obviously thought very highly of Anna, even though she was 'dumb', as you say. What attractions did you find in her that you didn't find in more educated people?

6. You speak very disapprovingly of 'cleverness', yet all our educations seems to be aimed at making us more clever. In what sense are you using this word? Or, to put it another way, what's wrong with cleverness?

7. The little man seems to have appeared more in your childhood than in your adolescence. What influences in your life tended to drive him away? Would it be right to assume that he appeared less and less as you grew older?

Class Conversation

What do you make of the little man in the passage? What aspect of Hermann Hesse's nature does the figure represent?

Think of a young child before it is capable of being taught anything. What can it do? What needs does it have? How does it show its character? Can you give some examples of the behaviour of small children? Perhaps your parents have described some of the things you did when you were very young.

When do we start 'blaming' children for what they do? Would you have blamed the young Hermann Hesse for some of the things he did?

We are born with certain instincts and impulses. What do we do 'instinctively'? Can instincts be changed or controlled? Are they the same in animals as in man?

To what extent are the following instinctive? Breathing, talking, eating, drinking, going to the toilet, swimming, blinking, laughing, crying, sleeping, writing, playing games, cooking food, dancing, protecting oneself?

What is the strongest instinct in living beings?

Is it instinctive for a woman to want to bear children? What do you think are the 'natural' roles of a mother and a father in a family? What do you think of as being a normal relationship between a child and its parents?

What makes people happy? What makes people wise? In the passage you have read, Anna is described as being happy and wise, yet she was also 'dumb'. Are educated people always happy and are they necessarily wise?

Word-study

Explain the meaning of the words printed in bold type in the following quotations from the passage and answer the additional questions.

1. *But of all the magic* **apparitions** (page 90, line 11)
   What is the meaning of *heir apparent*?
2. *I halfway* **exonerated** *myself* (page 91, line 17)
   Find the meaning of : *onus; onerous.*
3. *But the good, happy, lucky steps in my life . . . all occurred without* **reflection.**
   Which of the following meanings of *reflection* (page 92, line 17) is meant here:
   mirror image; unflattering comment; considered thought; reconsideration?
4. *she laughed loudly and* **immoderately** (page 92, line 26)
   Can you find two meanings for *moderation*?
5. *I* **chided** *her for this* (page 92, line 27)
6. *I explained it* **circumstantially** (page 92, line 36)
   The entry for *circumstantial* in the Concise Oxford Dictionary reads:
   Depending on subordinate details (*~evidence,* establishing

the doubtful main fact by inference from known facts otherwise hard to explain); adventitious, incidental; with many details (~*story*).
Which part of this definition applies to the word in the quotation?

7. *laughed quite madly and* **contagiously** (page 92, line 39)
What link is there between this word and *tangent, intangible, contiguous?*
8. *my friendship with Frau Anna had fallen into* **abeyance** (page 93, line 14)
9. *my eyes on the ground, unhappy and* **morose** (page 93, line 24)

Your own writing

1. Describe one or two young children that you know. Try to show their individual natures by giving examples of their behaviour and habits before they learn to 'do as they are told'.
2. Write a story about 'a spirit or goblin, angel or demon' who tempts people to change their natures and become the opposite of what they are normally. For instance, the strict, bad-tempered teacher could become lenient, the clever student could suddenly behave foolishly, the stay-at-home could be led into adventure, the miser might be tempted to give away all his money, the timid little mouse of a man could rise up and assert himself . . .! There are endless possibilities.
3. Write an essay or a short story about the difficulty of making an important decision in life. What choices are there? What factors influence the choice? What decision is made – and is it the right one?
4. Choose one aspect of the supernatural and write about it in the form of a story, an essay or a dialogue. There are many possibilities: apparitions, straightforward ghosts, weird creatures, inexplicable happenings in the night, spiritualism or former lives.
5. Give some examples of instinct operating in animals and birds or in human beings.
6. Choose one of the following titles to show how a character manages to survive in a difficult situation by using his skill and ingenuity:
   a) being attacked and chased by an animal or a person;

b) going in search of something or someone that is lost;

c) escaping in the nick of time.

7. Write about a friendship: how it began, how it developed and what it led to.

8. Select one of the topics from 'Class Conversation' and develop it into a piece of writing in any way you choose.

My Friend Havelock Ellis
Frank Ormsby

My first formal lesson on sex I owe
To my mother. Those faded books she bought
At the auction – sixpence the dozen, tied
With a rough string – hid one volume more
Than she bargained for.
For months I harboured him, forbidden one,
Under the green song sheets from *Ireland's Own*.

He never made the bookshelf, even wrapped
In a brown jacket. Consulted daily
Under clumps of trees beyond the hedge
That foiled the window's eye, his lectures turned
Often on mysteries.
I questioned him again until content
He'd yielded all, tutor and confidant.

Even in those days I knew at heart
How much he bored me. The tadpole-diagrams
He labelled Sperm, and cross-sections of organs
Like the cuts in butchers' windows, were less
Than living.
Still I intoned with a determined bliss
Words like fallopian, ovum, uterus.

The real joy was having such a friend,
Sure to be frowned on were his presence known.

He fed my independence, served a need
The set-texts neglected. Nothing left then
But to discard him;
Time for fresh schooling, lessons to begin
In the arms of my new friend, Rosita Quinn.

Considering the poem

1. What do you think the poem gains by referring to the book as *him?*
2. Why do you think the book was 'forbidden' and 'frowned upon'?
3. What does Frank Ormsby mean when he says he read the book:
   beyond the hedge
   That foiled the window's eye?
4. What suggests that the boy found parts of the book difficult to understand?
5. What difference is there between *tutor* and *confidant?*
6. What was the real satisfaction in possessing the book?

Talking and Writing

Choose one or more of the following questions for class conversation or personal writing.

In what ways do people of your own age become informed about human reproduction? Have you had sex education in your previous school or in the present one? How interesting and useful was it?

What do you think the role of parents ought to be in sex education?

Do you think the experience described in the poem is typical of young people and their parents today, or have attitudes changed since the poem was written?

If the human race has survived for thousands of years without formal sex education, why do you think it is necessary now?

Havelock Ellis 'served a need' for the young Frank Ormsby. Can you suggest what advantages and disadvantages there might be in studying this subject privately through one's own reading?

Seventeen Hours a Day
George Orwell

The *patron* had engaged me as a kitchen *plongeur*: that is, my job was to wash up, keep the kitchen clean, prepare vegetables, make tea, coffee and sandwiches, do the simpler cooking, and run errands. The terms were, as usual, five hundred francs a month and food, but I had no free day and no fixed working hours. At the Hotel X I had seen catering at its best, with unlimited money and good organisation. Now, at the Auberge, I learned how things are done in a thoroughly bad restaurant. It is worth describing, for there are hundreds of similar restaurants in Paris, and every visitor feeds in one of them occasionally.

I should add, by the way, that the Auberge was not the ordinary cheap eating-house frequented by students and workmen. We did not provide an adequate meal at less than twenty-five francs, and we were picturesque and artistic, which sent up our social standing. There were the indecent pictures in the bar, and the Norman decorations – sham beams on the walls, electric lights done up as candlesticks, 'peasant' pottery, even a mounting-block at the door – and the *patron* and the head waiter were Russian officers, and many of the customers titled Russian refugees. In short, we were decidedly chic.

Nevertheless, the conditions behind the kitchen door were suitable for a pigsty. For this is what our service arrangements were like.

The kitchen measured fifteen feet long by eight broad, and half this space was taken up by the stoves and the tables. All the pots had to be kept on shelves out of reach, and there was room for only one dustbin. This dustbin used to be crammed full by midday, and the floor was normally an inch deep in a compost of trampled food.

For firing we had nothing but three gas-stoves, without ovens, and all joints had to be sent out to the bakery.

There was no larder. Our substitute for one was a half-roofed shed in the yard, with a tree growing in the middle of it. The meat, vegetables and so forth lay there on the bare earth, raided by rats and cats.

There was no hot water laid on. Water for washing up had to be heated in pans, and, as there was no room for these on the stoves when meals were cooking, most of the plates had to be washed in cold water. This, with soft soap and the hard Paris water, meant scraping the grease off with bits of newspaper.

We were so short of saucepans that I had to wash each one as soon as it was done with, instead of leaving them till the evening. This alone probably wasted an hour a day.

Owing to some scamping of expense in the installation, the electric light usually fused at eight in the evening. The *patron* would only allow us three candles in the kitchen, and the cook said three were unlucky, so we had only two.

Our coffee-grinder was borrowed from a *bistro* near by, and our dustbin and brooms from the concierge. After the first week a quantity of linen did not come back from the wash, as the bill was not paid. We were in trouble with the inspector of labour, who had discovered that the staff included no Frenchmen; he had several private interviews with the *patron,* who, I believe, was obliged to bribe him. The electric company was still dunning us, and when the duns found that we would buy them off with apéritifs, they came every morning. We were in debt at the grocery, and credit would have been stopped, only the grocer's wife (a moustachio'd woman of sixty) had taken a fancy to Jules, who was sent every morning to cajole her. Similarly I had to waste an hour every day haggling over vegetables in the rue du Commerce, to save a few centimes.

These are the results of starting a restaurant on insufficient capital. And in these conditions the cook and I were expected to serve thirty or forty meals a day, and would later on be serving a hundred. From the first day it was too much for us. The cook's working hours were from eight in the morning till midnight, and mine from seven in the morning till half past twelve the next morning – seventeen and a half hours, almost without a break. We never had time to sit down till five in the afternoon, and even then there was no seat except the top of the dustbin. Boris, who lived near by and had not to catch the last Métro home, worked from eight in the morning till two the next morning – eighteen hours a day, seven days a week. Such hours, though not unusual, are nothing extraordinary in Paris.

Life settled at once into a routine that made the Hotel X seem like a holiday. Every morning at six I drove myself out of bed, did not shave, sometimes washed, hurried up to the Place d'Italie and fought for a place on the Métro. By seven I was in the desolation of the cold, filthy kitchen, with the potato skins and bones and fishtails littered on the floor, and a pile of plates, stuck together in their grease, waiting from overnight. I could not start on the plates yet, because the water was cold, and I had to fetch milk and make coffee, for the others arrived at eight and expected to find coffee ready. Also, there were always several copper saucepans to clean. Those copper saucepans are the bane of a *plongeur's* life. They have to be scoured with sand and bunches of chain, ten minutes to each one, and then polished on the outside with Brasso. Fortunately, the art of making them has been lost and they are gradually vanishing from French kitchens, though one can still buy them second-hand.

When I had begun on the plates the cook would take me away from the plates to begin skinning onions, and when I had begun on the onions the *patron* would arrive and send me out to buy cabbages. When I came back with the cabbages the *patron's* wife would tell me to go to some shop half a mile away and buy a pot of rouge; by the time I came back there would be more vegetables waiting, and the plates were still not done. In this way our incompetence piled one job on another throughout the day, everything in arrears.

Till ten, things went comparatively easily, though we were work-ing fast, and no one lost his temper. The cook would find time to talk about her artistic nature, and say did I not think Tolstoy was *épat-ant,* and sing in a fine soprano voice as she minced beef on the board. But at ten the waiters began clamouring for their lunch, which they had early, and at eleven the first customers would be arriving. Sud-denly everything became hurry and bad temper. There was not the same furious rushing and yelling as at the Hotel X, but an atmos-phere of muddle, petty spite and exasperation. Discomfort was at the bottom of it. It was unbearably cramped in the kitchen, and dishes had to be put on the floor, and one had to be thinking constantly about not stepping on them. The cook's vast buttocks banged against me as she moved to and fro. A ceaseless, nagging chorus of orders streamed from her:

'Unspeakable idiot! How many times have I told you not to bleed the beetroots? Quick, let me get to the sink! Put those knives away; get on with the potatoes. What have you done with my strainer? Oh, leave those potatoes alone. Didn't I tell you to skim the *bouillon*? Take that can of water off the stove. Never mind the washing up, chop this celery. No, not like that, you fool, like this. There! Look at you letting those peas boil over! Now get to work and scale those herrings. Look, do you call this plate clean? Wipe it on your apron. Put that salad on the floor. That's right, put it where I'm bound to step in it. Look out, that pot's boiling over! Get me down that saucepan. No, the other one. Put this on the grill. Throw those potatoes away. Don't waste time, throw them on the floor. Tread them in. Now throw down some sawdust; this floor's like a skating rink. Look, you fool that steak's burning! *Mon Dieu,* why did they send me an idiot for a *plongeur*? Who are you talking to? Do you realise that my aunt was a Russian countess?' etc. etc. etc.

This went on till three o'clock without much variation, except that about eleven the cook usually had a *crise de nerfs* and a flood of tears. From three to five was a fairly slack time for the waiters, but the cook was still busy, and I was working my fastest, for there was a pile of dirty plates waiting, and it was a race to get them done, or partly done, before dinner began. The washing up was doubled by the primitive conditions – a cramped draining-board, tepid water, sodden cloths, and a sink that got blocked once in an hour. By five the cook and I were feeling unsteady on our feet, not having eaten or sat down since seven. We used to collapse, she on the dustbin and I on the floor, drink a bottle of beer, and apologise for some of the things we had said in the morning. Tea was what kept us going. We took care to have a pot always stewing, and drank pints during the day.

At half-past five the hurry and quarrelling began again, and now worse than before, because everyone was tired. The cook had a *crise de nerfs* at six and another at nine; they came on so regularly that one could have told the time by them. She would flop down on the dustbin, begin weeping hysterically, and cry out that never, no, never had she thought to come to such a life as this; her nerves would not stand it; she had studied music in Vienna; she had a

bedridden husband to support, etc. etc. At another time one would
have been sorry for her, but, tired as we all were, her whimpering
voice merely infuriated us. Jules used to stand in the doorway and
mimic her weeping. The *patron's* wife nagged, and Boris and Jules
quarrelled all day, because Jules shirked his work, and Boris, as
head waiter, claimed the larger share of the tips. Only the second
day after the restaurant opened, they came to blows in the kitchen
over a two-franc tip, and the cook and I had to separate them. The
only person who never forgot his manners was the *patron*. He kept
the same hours as the rest of us, but he had no work to do, for it was
his wife who really managed things. His sole job, besides ordering
the supplies, was to stand in the bar smoking cigarettes and looking
gentlemanly, and he did that to perfection.

The cook and I generally found time to eat our dinner between ten
and eleven o'clock. At midnight the cook would steal a packet of food
for her husband, stow it under her clothes, and make off, whimpering that these hours would kill her and she would give notice in the
morning. Jules also left at midnight, usually after a dispute with
Boris, who had to look after the bar till two. Between twelve and
half past I did what I could to finish the washing up. There was no
time to attempt doing the work properly, and I used simply to rub
the grease off the plates with table-napkins. As for the dirt on the
floor, I let it lie, or swept the worst of it out of sight under the stoves.

At half past twelve I would put on my coat and hurry out. The
patron, bland as ever, would stop me as I went down the alley-way
past the bar. '*Mais, mon cher monsieur,* how tired you look! Please,
do me the favour of accepting this glass of brandy.'

He would hand me the glass of brandy as courteously as though I
had been a Russian duke instead of a *plongeur*. He treated all of us
like this. It was our compensation for working seventeen hours a
day.

As a rule the last Métro was almost empty – a great advantage,
for one could sit down and sleep for a quarter of an hour. Generally I
was in bed by half past one. Sometimes I missed the train and had to
sleep on the floor of the restaurant, but it hardly mattered, for I
could have slept on cobblestones at that time.

(from *Down and Out in Paris and London*)

The Interview

Imagine that you are George Orwell and that you are being inteviewed about your work in the restaurant. What would you say in answer to these questions?

1. Do you think it was wise to accept a job in which you had no free day and no fixed working hours?
2. The *patron* had obviously spent a lot of money on the restaurant, but nothing at all on the kitchen. Was this good business, do you think?
3. You are a bit sarcastic when you describe the restaurant as 'artistic'. What was wrong with the decor and the taste?
4. The long hours worked by the staff must have had a serious effect on them. What effect did it have on the cook, for instance? And yourself?
5. As you were the menial in the kitchen, everybody seemed to be making use of you – even the *patron's* wife, who sent you to buy make-up for her. Didn't you feel like protesting?
6. Can you summarize how your relationship with the cook fluctuated throughout the day – according to how busy you were?
7. Would you agree that you couldn't think of the cook impartially because you were so caught up in the squabbles that arose from working in such terrible conditions? Looking back on that situation, what do you think of the cook now?
8. You say that the *patron* never forgot his manners and imply that it was because he had no work to do. Do you think, then, that good manners are possible only when people are not involved in hard work? Or can good manners still exist in difficult working conditions?

Word-study

1. It is not surprising that there are several French expressions in the passage. Can you find out the meaning of:
   patron (page 100, line 1), *plongeur* (page 100, line 1), *auberge* (page 100, line 7), *chic* (page 100, line 20), *bistro* (page 101, line 21), *concierge* (page 101, line 22), *apéritif* (page 101, line 28), *rue de Commerce* (page 101, line 33), *Métro* (page 102, line 3), *épatant* (page 102, line 32), *bouillon* (page 103, line 7),

Mon Dieu (page 103, line 17), *crise de nerfs* (page 103, line 21), *Mais, mon cher monsieur* (page 104, line 26)

2. Write out the following phrases or sentences and after each one explain the meaning of the word in bold type:
   frequented *by students* (page 100, line 12), **sham** *beams* (page 100, line 16), **scamping** *of expense* (page 101, line 17), *the electric company was still* **dunning** *us* (page 101, line 27), *to* **cajole** *her* (page 101, line 31), *insufficient* **capital** (page 101, line 34), *the* **bane** *of a plongeur's life* (page 102, line 17), **tepid** *water* (page 103, line 26) *the patron,* **bland** *as ever* (page 104, line 24)

Class Conversation

It is interesting that Orwell's relationship with the cook fluctuated throughout the day and that in the evening they used to apologise to each other for the things they had said in the morning. In other words, they didn't really mean what they had said. Is it your experience that people who have rows usually make it up afterwards? Or do the rows drag on?

Have you ever been in a situation in which you have considered yourself to be overworked? What did you do about it? Or what would you like to have done about it?

Orwell says: *Every morning at six I drove myself out of bed, did not shave, sometimes washed . . .*
Are you good at getting up, or do you often sleep in? Has anything terrible happened when you have overslept? On what occasions are you willing to get up very early?

Orwell obviously hated the mess and disorder in the kitchen, but could do little about it. People can often be divided into those who fuss about untidiness and those who are indifferent to it. Which are you? How do you look after your own room at home?

The cook's working hours were from eight in the morning till midnight, and mine from seven in the morning till half past twelve the next morning . . .
What do you think of such working hours? What is the longest day you have worked? What is the longest you have stayed awake?

The passage takes you 'behind the scenes' at a fashionable restaurant. You have probably only experienced the customer's side of things. What are your feelings when you go into a restaurant? Any amusing or embarrassing incidents to relate?

Do you find working in the kitchen at home enjoyable or tedious? What jobs in the kitchen do you like best – and least?

Orwell's 'slavery' as a *plongeur* is a perfect illustration of the need for a trade union to prevent the exploitation of workers. Do you agree?

Your own writing

1. Write your response to three or four of the topics in 'Class Conversation'.
2. Write a play on the subject of washing-up. You could divide up your play into short scenes, which might be concerned with: the argument about who does the washing-up; the exchanges that take place during the washing-up; one or two dramatic or humorous incidents; the final tidying up. Choose two or three characters and make them clearly defined, with a distinctive way of speaking. The setting could be at home, in a café or hotel, in a youth hostel, in a caravan, at a party – wherever washing-up has to be done!
3. What arguments can be put forward for a) people being allowed to work as many hours a day or a week as they wish; b) people's working hours being restricted by law? Choose your examples from particular occupations.
4. Imagine that, either now or in the future, you are completely broke – penniless! You need money to live on and you have to get a job soon. (Let's assume that there is no social security to help you over your bad patch!)
   Tell the story of the job, or jobs, you eventually found and how you managed to survive.
5. Think of the orders you are given throughout a typical day, both at school, at work and at home. Compose a paragraph, similar to the cook's string of orders to George Orwell, of all the things you are told to do during one day.
6. You have a foreign friend who is about to visit this country and

who will be travelling widely. Give him or her some idea of
what to expect from British cafés and restaurants: their variety, their appearance, the food that is served, the service and
the prices.

Schoolday
Stanley Cook

Half-past six: the badly balanced alarm clock
Falls over in its excitement. My dressing gown
And slippers happen to me. The light on the landing,
Still left on all night though our younger daughter
Is growing old enough to dream of boys
Instead of bogeys, focusses my eyes
And Monday struggles with my whole mechanism.

Downstairs, in the all-night burner the buds of coal
Flower like furze in the draught as I open the front.
The children come down: 'Where is my dinner money,
Shirt, swimming trunks, other shoe,
Greek, Latin, French, English book,
Bug rake?' The door slams, a bolt falling out, behind them.

Last, I begin, for the two thousandth time and more,
Past the affected scruffiness of students
And professional prettiness of office girls
At the bus stops, my ten minute walk to school,
Not even a puddle of which is my private property.

The usual people tell the time by me
And I tell the time by them. An audience
Of trees come up from the country watch from a wood
Or themselves mime in the breeze; banks mailed
With ivy leaves shake their spears of seeded grass
While the sound of commuter traffic opens and shuts.

In the schoolyard the jigsaw of waiting boys
Is nearly finished, some cheeky or polite enough
To say good morning, some without a mac or coat
Whatever the weather. Pausing in the staffroom
I glance through 'The Guardian' for news that fits
My Monday view of the world: SKELETON
DISCOVERED IN EDUCATION OFFICE CUPBOARD.
RESEARCH CONFIRMS WHAT ANYONE WITH SENSE
ALREADY KNEW.

       Then along the aquarian gloom
Of the low corridors to register my form,
The identical boys I have taught for twenty years
But calling themselves each year by different names.
I prop up present marks for the best of friends
And the bully and his victim, more together
In their schooldays than they will ever be again.

From lesson to lesson their feelings rain on the ruins
Of Chaucer and Shakespeare, whose characters, did they but see,
Teach them this very day, the sanguine Scoutmaster,
Red-cheeked and weather-beaten to the white margin
Of forehead covered by his scout-hat band,
And the lean industrious scholar, tonsured by baldness,
Picking out a prepositional idiom
Like a speck from an eye with a handkerchief corner,
Came back here from Canterbury. Hamlet,
Postponing his life till he gets a better job,
Sits in the staffroom, gleaning last week's *Times Ed.,*
Or in his forties is resigned as Antony
To his being passed over for a younger man.
I am the gutter my form's perceptions run down.

Break: I sniff the jugs of cocoa and coffee
To tell which is which; dregs gather in balls at the bottom
Of the plastic cup. The school bell twangles too soon.

Then twelve: no wonder they spell it 'dinning room'.
'Stop behaving like an idiot.'
                      'But, sir, I am an idiot.'

'Don't be childish.'
　　　　　　　　'But, sir, I am a child.'
Poetry in the afternoon:
Love poems by a seducer and adulterer,
Humour by an attempted suicide.
Authors apparently matter as little as teachers
For time eventually turns up in my pupils' minds
Ideals appropriate to their age
Intelligence and environment.

Late enough at break for the afternoon tea
For a taste of the sugar from the teapot bottom.

Last period at last. (Why are the boys
Who talk so much the worst at oral work?)
And four o'clock: a gargle of corridor duty
Rinses out the loitering first formers
Humping homework and swags of football kit:
All stretched, if you troubled to measure them,
A little taller in the course of the day.

Considering the poem

1. Which statements in the first verse seem to you to convey very
   well the difficulty of waking up and getting up on a Monday
   morning?
2. What do you understand by *the affected scruffiness of students*?
3. What is the poet suggesting the ivy leaves look like when he
   says that the banks are 'mailed' by them? Which phrase con-
   tinues this metaphor?
4. What does *The Guardian* headline mean?
5. The teachers in the school are compared to characters from
   Chaucer and Shakespeare. Can you say briefly what is charac-
   teristic of the teachers referred to as: the Scoutmaster, the scholar, Hamlet, Antony?
6. What does Stanley Cook mean when he describes himself as *the
   gutter my form's perceptions run down*?
7. Why does he think *authors apparently matter as little as
   teachers* to his pupils?
8. What would you say were Stanley Cook's moods throughout the

day, judging by the comments he makes? Can you give some examples?

9. Quote some examples of incidents, characters, conversations or details which strike you as being very true to life.
10. There are several figures of speech in the poem – personification, metaphor and simile in particular. Quote some examples and say which you think are most effective.

Your own writing

The structure of the poem follows the pattern of the day: getting up, incidents in the house before the children leave, the walk to school, registration, lessons, break, dinner, afternoon lessons, the end of the school day. It is a pattern we all recognise because we have all experienced something similar. The verses vary in length and are similar to paragraphs in a composition, each one concerned with a separate aspect of the day. Throughout, we are conscious of the poet-teacher himself: his changing moods, his comments on other people, his dry humour, his sudden shifts from colloquial language to the figurative expressions of poetry. We really get to know him during his school day.

Think of a typical day in your own life. How do you go through it – or part of it? What do you do, how do you feel, what do you observe about your surroundings and about other people? What pattern emerges? It need not be a school day – it could be a day at your job, a Saturday morning or evening, a Sunday, a holiday, a day off, a birthday, the day of an important event.

Describe your day in verse form, a verse for each main incident or development. Bring in description and conversation if you wish; and make your writing lively and imaginative. At the end of the poem, we may have got to know you better.

Dinner at the Castle
Gavin Maxwell

In the Christmas holidays after my fifteenth birthday we all went to
stay with my Aunt and Uncle Northumberland at Alnwick Castle
for the Hunt Ball. Of the thirty or forty guests I was by several years
the youngest; I was also the only one possessing neither a tail-coat,
dinner-jacket, nor the least grain of savoir-faire. The mores of what
is now called Establishment life were as foreign to me as the rules
and conventions of my first school had been, for my whole upbringing had represented a seccession from precisely this background.
Moreover, I was now of an age when the desperate desire to conform
and be accepted socially gave rise to greater mental anguish than
could ever be known to a ten-year-old. There was no one to instruct
me; my brother had little more experience than I, and my mother,
though this had been her home, knew only the female side of life,
and in Victorian and Edwardian days at that.

Even after all these years I can hardly write of my major gaffe
without experiencing again something of the agony it caused me
then; thinking of it I shrink to fit that subfusc suit that was my
garment of shame; reliving it my heart reaches out with a gush of
compassion to all who know the dreadful uncertainties of adolescence, the tormented confusion of social failure. There were three
incidents in one evening, and by the third I had become incapable of
speech or rational behaviour.

I had a bath before dinner – early, because I was determined that
at least I would not be late down to the drawing-room. I dawdled in
the bath, because I realized that in my zeal for punctuality I had
overdone it, and that I should have more than half an hour to put

away. Blissfully unaware that I had left the bathroom door unlocked, I lay in the shallow water with my back to it, idly twirling my pubic hair into two neat little buffalo horns with a parting down the centre. The door opened. Instead of performing any conventional gesture of modesty I scrambled precipitately to my feet and turned to face the sound. I found myself confronting in all my bizarre nudity a very pretty blond girl of about twenty, clothed in an elaborately frilly pink dressing-gown and carrying a bath-towel over her arm. Whereas my own reactions to the situation had been so very inappropriate, hers might have been scripted for her by a ham playwright. She gasped, turned scarlet as her eyes took in my nether coiffure; she said: 'Heavens!' in a steam-engine whisper, and her free hand went up to cover her mouth. Then she was gone with a slam of the door. My very first action, even before locking the door, was comparable to that of a child who has been caught writing something obscene on a blackboard – I rubbed it out. That is to say I seized a towel and scrubbed my bush back to normal, as if it were responsible for the whole incident. Then I spent ten minutes in the bathroom not daring to go back to my room lest I should meet her in the passage. Dressing, I was obsessed by the needling knowledge that there was a girl in the house who knew just what I looked like without any clothes on, and by the idea that she would tell all her friends and giggle about it. It didn't occur to me that it might have been quite a pleasurable experience for her, or that there was nothing unusual or unpleasant about my body.

I found my way to the drawing-room. It was empty, but for an enormous butler who stood in the entrance carrying a silver salver. As I approached him he advanced upon me, proffering the salver in complete silence. My inspection of it was cursory; I did not dare to hesitate and thus display my ignorance. A rapid, furtive glance had shown me that the tray was covered with folded white cards, each standing like two playing-cards propped together as the first stage of a card castle. None of them appeared to have anything written on it. I was clearly required to take one, so I treated it as a sort of lucky-dip; I closed my eyes firmly and took one at random.

The butler showed no surprise, and withdrew. I went on into the drawing-room, and when I was certain that I was alone I cautiously examined what I had taken. On the outside – the side, presumably, that had faced away from me – was written 'Captain George Babington-Smith', and on the inside 'Please take Lady Anne Egerton in to dinner'. A tremor of something like giddiness swept over me. The fact that there could be no way of escaping detection did not immediately strike me; as in the bathroom, my first instinct was to expunge the outward and visible sign, and I hurried to throw the evidence into the fire. It was only after I had done so that I began to be racked by guilt. I had made an irreparable muddle; the romance between Captain Babington-Smith and Lady Anne Egerton, of which I knew, would be shattered because of my clumsiness, and I could think of no way of putting things right. I began to rehearse what I might say to him when he came down: 'Captain Babington-Smith,' I would say with a charmingly insouciant smile, 'I'm terribly sorry but I'm afraid I took your card by mistake,' – but then I realised that by burning the card I had made all explanation impossible. I waited miserably, saying little prayers to myself that what I had done might be undone. Then it occurred to me that because the butler had presented the salver to me there obviously must be somebody whom I was supposed to take in to dinner, and I had no means of finding out who it was. I skulked in a distant corner of the drawing-room while the guests congregated; I saw the girl who had come into the bathroom and I edged to keep out of her sight; presently I spotted the couple whom I had sundered, talking cheerfully together as though my prayers had been answered and the Lord had wiped clean the slate of the last half-hour. My ears must have been twitching like a rabbit's, straining for the least word from any quarter that would betray knowledge of my secret. A raddled old lady who cannot have been less than eighty, plastered with make-up, crusted and collared with diamonds, darted a snake-like glance at me and I caught her emery-paper attempt at a whisper. 'Such an attractive-looking boy, but they say he's so shy.'

(Later I repeated this to my sister, omitting the latter half of the sentence and adding: 'I'm going to make a collection of all the nice things that have ever been said about me, and publish it.' She replied: 'And I shall make a collection of all the nasty things that have been said about you, twice as long, and publish that.' I was easily deflated.) Time dragged on; the rest of my family arrived but I shunned them, waiting miserably for the denouement that would come when dinner was announced. It came with the anti-climax of a time-bomb with a dud fuse; the guests went in in pairs, Captain Babington-Smith with Lady Anne Egerton, and I, with no partner, slunk in last.

I sat between two young men in pink coats who talked only with the girls at their other sides. I was grateful for this, but at the same time it seemed yet another indignity that in the seating arrangements I should be treated as a girl and in the event as one unworthy of notice.

My final shame was still to come. Quite early on in the meal my knife slipped on the plate and a large green pea shot into the middle of the table, leaving an irregular spoor of gravy behind it. There it lay, seeming to me as big as a football, while course succeeded course and the footmen ignored it with studious spite. It was still there when they cleared everything else away and brought the dessert-plates; it was still there when the ladies left the room and I was able to move a few places up the table and disown it for ever.

I moved up and sat next to Aymer, who, though I did not guess it, was feeling very nearly as insecure as I was. My uncle, however, did guess it, and with a gesture of kindness which I shall always remember he left his place at the distant head of the table and came all the way down to sit beside us in his resplendent pink coat, and to talk to us as if we were the most important of all his guests. From that moment I didn't care what 'Janitor' thought of him; he joined my heroes, and when he died suddenly, only nine months later, I wished miserably that I had even been able to tell him how grateful I had been.

Among all the works on adolescent psychology that I have read I have not found one whose author seems to remember what it is like to be an adolescent. They state academic truths, but the standpoint is external, as detached as if they were recording experimental data on the behaviour of laboratory rats, and no one can remember what it feels like to be a laboratory rat. The abyss that gapes between the average adult and the average adolescent is not fundamentally a failure of knowledge – though that, too, exists in the great majority of cases – but a failure of understanding that is less excusable, for it is due to a wilful, often compulsive forgetfulness. Pavlov found that he could produce anxiety states in dogs by creating conditions of uncertainty. Most adolescents live in a perpetual state of uncertainty, and therefore of anxiety, because of an immutable attitude in their elders towards what is, for the adolescent, a mutable set of circumstances. The normal adolescent revolt against authority is not, as I see and remember it, a challenge to the existence of the boss figures – who are more necessary now than they have ever been before – but a protest against their inadequacy, their failure in elasticity; in short simply their failure to remember. In particular, their failure to remember that values which have become absolute to them are not so to the adolescent. In adult terms cancer of the brain is of more absolute significance than pimples on the face, future bankruptcy of more absolute importance than the present wearing of unsuitable clothes. These concepts are meaningless to the emoting adolescent; the pimples and the unsuitable clothes may cause him the greatest amount of disturbance of which he believes himself capable, and they are therefore obstacles in his path as monstrous as cancer or bankruptcy to the adult. If he measured the importance of any circumstance or happening he would do so only in measurement units of his own disturbance, not by any absolute standards that are the product of environment and experience.

So the muddle that I had produced that evening seemed to me as great, and the consequences as appalling, as any international crisis can ever have appeared to a statesman whose ineptitude had produced it. True, I didn't actually contemplate suicide, but very few boys do, and I should say even fewer eminent statesmen.

(from *The House of Elrig*)

The Interview

Write the answers to the questions as though you were the author himself, using the information that is given in the passage and what you can reasonably deduce from it.

1. Generally speaking, what was your main cause for concern at going to the Hunt Ball?
2. Do you think now – on looking back – that the mistakes you made were really important?
3. You say your reaction to the girl coming into the bathroom was *very inappropriate*. Perhaps it was, but what else could you have done?
4. You obviously panicked over the card when you threw it on the fire. Why were you in such a state? What would you have done if you had been more self-confident and cool-headed?
5. Do you think the footmen were ignoring the pea out of spite?
6. You criticize adults rather severely. What would you say is their worst fault in their relations with younger people?

G

7. Your uncle seems to have been an exception. Why did you feel so grateful to him that evening?
8. To what extent were you yourself to blame for the agony you suffered that evening?

Class Conversation

Gavin Maxwell was unprepared for the society he was moving in at Alnwick Castle and behaved awkwardly. What social occasions have you attended at which you were expected to behave in a certain way? Were you conscious of social failure or social success?

Most people are shy at some time in their lives. Have you outgrown shyness (if you ever *were* shy), or is it still there? On what sort of occasion, or with which particular people, do you find yourself being shy or awkward? Why do you behave like this?

When you read the description of the incident in the bathroom, what was your reaction? A person's attitude to nudity probably comes from his upbringing and the society he lives in. Discuss the tolerance of – and the objections to – nudity in some of the following situations: on beaches, in advertisements, in films and in the theatre, in art, amongst primitive people, in newspapers and magazines.

'Good manners' take on a lot of importance for some people. Children are told to 'behave themselves', to be 'on their best behaviour' and to 'mind their p's and q's'. What 'manners' – table or otherwise – were you taught as a child? Are they necessary and useful? Will you teach your children 'good manners' when you are a parent?

Can you give some examples from your own experience of what adults consider important and you consider unimportant? Or vice versa?

Speeches and sketches

Most men and many women at some time in their lives are called upon to make a speech, usually on a social occasion such as a wedding reception, a club dinner, a presentation or a retirement. The

speeches tend to be light-hearted and entertaining, spiced with jokes, anecdotes and quotations, and flattering or satirical in their references to people present. In order to prepare yourself for one of these occasions, write and deliver a speech by one of the following:
  the bridegroom *or* the best-man *or* the father of the bride *or* a favourite uncle at a wedding reception;
  a headmaster on the retirement of a member of staff *or* the retiring teacher himself/herself;
  a guest speaker at a club dinner *or* the chairman who proposes a vote of thanks;
  any speaker at a school's Speech Day.

Write or improvise a sketch based on a family of four having a meal in a restaurant. Plan the development of the sketch and consider introducing such features as: deciding where to sit; choosing the meal; mishaps with food, drink and cutlery; table manners; family moods and tempers; complaints; footing the bill – and whatever other incidents might enliven the sketch.

Devise a sketch in which a mother instructs her (unco-operative?) children in table manners – starting with sitting down and going through each course of the meal until it is time to 'leave the table'. You might include such things as: waiting to begin, how to drink soup quietly, how to hold knives and forks, what to 'eat up', how to sit, what noises you shouldn't make – and many other rules with which you are probably all too familiar.

Word-study

Use a dictionary for this part of the work, but make sure that the definition you select applies to the meaning of the word in the passage. Write out the following phrases and after each one give a definition of the word or words in bold type:

  page 113 *nor the least grain of* **savoir-faire** *(line 5); the* **mores** *of what is now called Establishment life (line 5);* **conventions** *of my first school (line 7); a* **secession** *from precisely this background (line 8); my major* **gaffe** (line 15); **rational** *behaviour* (line 22); *my* **zeal** *for punctuality* (line 25);

page 114: *I scrambled* **precipitately** *to my feet* (line 5); *my* **bizarre** *nudity* (line 6); *a silver* **salver** (line 27); *my inspection of it was* **cursory** (line 29); *a rapid,* **furtive** *glance* (line 30); *took one* **at random** (line 35);

page 115: *to* **expunge** *the outward and visible sign* (line 3); *an* **irreparable** *muddle* (line 6); *a charming* **insouciant** *smile* (line 11); *I* **skulked** *in a distant corner* (line 18); *a* **raddled** *old lady* (line 25); *the* **denouement** *that would come* (line 36);

page 116: *an irregular* **spoor** *of gravy* (line 8); *in his* **resplendent** *pink coat* (line 18); *the* **abyss** *that gapes* (line 29); **compulsive** *forgetfulness* (line 33); *an* **immutable** *attitude* (line 36);

page 117: *whose* **ineptitude** *had produced it* (line 17).

Your own writing

1. What we say is not always what we think; and what we think we don't always express. Write out the *thoughts* of a person attending a social occasion such as a wedding ceremony, a presentation of prizes, a party, a bingo session or a break during working hours.

2. Write a short story about a character who is either determined to ignore social politenesses or who knows nothing at all about them. Put your character into a situation which required 'correct' behaviour. What happens?

3. Imagine, during a journey of exploration (in time or in space), you come across a strange community of people who have remained unknown to modern civilisation and who have none of the attitudes, manners or customs of our own society. Describe your visit to this community and give an account of the unusual way of life to be found there.

4. Make a collection of *a*) the nice things people could say and *b*) the nasty things people could say about *either* yourself *or* a person you know *or* an imaginary character *or* a character you have read about.

5. Write a short play or dialogue in which a person from one social class (with the accent and style of speech that go with it) encounters a person of a contrasting social class (with the style of speech to match).

6. 'Most adolescents live in a state of perpetual uncertainty.' If you think this is true, describe some of the problems and uncertainties of a typical adolescent.
7. Write on some of the points discussed in 'Class Conversation'.

All Night Disco
Wes Magee

Against
     knife-like lights my eyes peel like ripe plums
and the white strobe is timed to make you vomit.
Death sounds shriek and squeal to the wild, bucking floor,
amoebas of paint coagulate on walls
and, yes, we move on the bed of some rank pond.

     The girls
          joggle bodies in isolation
faces white as cut loaves, fingernails purpled
as if they've plundered damsons in the Ladies.
Disorientation's the pain of the game
and as a torture room this takes some beating.

     The men
          sidling like weary hunters, stalk flesh
while I grip a drink and cling to the swamped bar.
Cosmic with noise the ceiling aches to faint
as someone flops from a chair like a wet sack.
The groovers, stoned with sound, lurch towards dawn.

     Outside
the night's hard dreams
fall to the streets
     as rain.

Considering the poem

1. Would you say that the language of the poem is predominantly literal or figurative?
2. Which images suggest the physical revulsion Wes Magee feels?
3. Which images express the uncanny, surrealistic atmosphere of the disco?
4. Since sound obviously plays an important part in a disco, do you think the nature of the sound has been effectively conveyed in the poem? Quote relevant lines in your answer.
5. What evidence is there in the poem to suggest that (according to the poet) the dancers are not really enjoying themselves?
6. Can you explain what is being expressed or implied in the last verse of the poem?
7. The poem is written in free verse, but there is a certain pattern or structure to it. Can you say what this is?
8. What do you think of the poem?

Your own writing

Attempt a poem or a prose description that stresses the atmosphere of a place and your reactions to it. You also could choose a disco and, without imitating the language of the poem, describe the sounds, the lighting effects, the behaviour of the dancers and, above all, your feelings and sensations whilst there, using figurative language – similes, metaphors and personification – to make your writing more vivid.

But you may not want to write about a disco. Choose, then, a similar subject, such as a dance hall, a party, a crowded gathering, a pop concert or a rally. Using the technique of description allied to an expression of personal feelings, try to give your impression of what it was like to be there.

At Sixteen
Winifred Foley

Nature had been trying hard to push me into womanhood, and she was having a bit of a struggle. Now, after half a year on the farm, she was eventually winning. A frugal but healthy diet, plenty of exercise, sound sleep, early rising, early bed, no worries, and the fresh air from the mountains filling the lungs by day and night. It had its effect; I was blossoming out very roundly in the right places: a fact that, unknown to me, hadn't escaped the watchful eye of the young man who owned the next farm. He had even wasted his time hanging about on his land next to the lane, to watch me on my weekly walk to the shop.

If his name cropped up at the farm, my mistress gave a disapproving sniff, for he was known as 'a bit of a wild lad' who rode a motorbike, and stayed out half the night in Abergavenny town. He was twenty-six.

I had been allowed to go into Abergavenny once for a spending spree, with three-months saved-up wages. I sent a postal order home to Mam, and had plenty left for shoes and a few everyday clothes, plus a pale-green silk dress and a wide-brimmed lacy straw hat with green ribbons. When the year was up, and I due for a holiday, I intended to impress the boys back home. Then an unexpected opportunity came for me to wear my new finery.

Two things happened. The old man went off to stay with another son, and the new chapel minister invited my master and mistress to stay on after Sunday evening service, and to take supper with him.

These blessings put my mistress in such a transport of good humour that she told me I could have time off to go to Sunday-evening chapel. Poor Bert would have to be the Christian who did all the chores! 'Six days shalt thou labour' had to be overlooked in his case.

Normally, I'd have preferred to stay at home and help Bert rather than listen to a Sunday sermon, but I wasn't going to miss the chance to try out my new clothes. Saturday morning I washed my hair and put it in curling papers.

The master and mistress, with the baby, started for chapel well ahead of me, which gave me the chance to pinch a dab of her Pond's Vanishing Cream to put on my snub nose. As I looked in her mirror, I blushed rose-pink with pleasure. Oh, it couldn't be me! That pretty girl, in a lovely dress, with brown silky curls, and round face framed in lacy straw!

Bert was so surprised he nearly stepped back into the bucket of pig-swill he'd been stirring. He looked quite hungry at the sight of me.

Freedom to walk out in the hedgerowed lane normally meant that I would indulge in a hop-skip-and-dance routine when out of sight of the farm. But today I walked proud and sedate like a young lady of quality.

On the very corner of the lane was a farmhouse that looked in the front as grand as a manor, although the back was the usual quagmire surrounded by barns, stables, and pig-styes. Just as I passed, a girl about my own age picked her way carefully to the gate. She was carrying a Bible, and was obviously in her Sunday clothes. Not having seen her before, I didn't venture to speak. She, however, had seen me often as I carried the paraffin, and knew that I was the 'help' at Little Rowan Farm. She did similar work on a grander scale. She was Welsh and friendly, and talkative. Her dad was a miner too, in Abertillery. She was the eldest of six, and her name was Letty Meadows. We had a lot in common, except that I thought her name and herself much prettier than I.

The chapel was a mile further on past the village. It was a minute building of grey stone, not important enough to have its own churchyard, but set in a neat grass plot just off the road. It was almost filled. Considering the sparseness of the local population, it proved how popular chapel attending was in Wales.

The service had not yet begun. My master and mistress were up front, talking to the new minister. Filled with gracious superiority by the minister's attention, my mistress beckoned me to her and

introduced me as 'our maid'. I thought the description savoured of
swank, and wasn't in the spirit of Jesus as taught in chapel. I was
glad to return to Letty on the back seat by the door.

She was no more interested in the sermon than I was; neither
were a couple of likeable-looking lads, in the seat in front of us, who
weren't taken in by the apparent indifference Letty and I showed to
their head-turnings in our direction.

'I wonder if they'll follow us after,' whispered Letty hopefully.

In unspoken agreement, we didn't hang around the chapel door,
but hurried off down the road, to escape surveillance by our elders.

'Don't turn round, but, indeed, they are following us,' said Letty,
well pleased.

Gauche and unsure like dog puppies, bold and diffident by turns,
they whistled the popular love ballads of the day to us, and shouted
out compliments disguised as sarcasm.

We answered and encouraged them in the only ways we knew –
tossing our curls, giggling to each other, and even looking round to
acknowledge their presence. Suddenly, a tuppenny bar of chocolate
fell, from mid-air, in front of our feet.

'Which one do you like best?' asked Letty. Highly flattered at
getting any masculine attention at all, I didn't feel too fussy; also it
was most likely that they were both after Letty. So, to be on the safe
side, I lied, 'I don't fancy either of 'em.'

After about half a mile, the boys had got up to within a few feet of
us; but they hung back a bit when they saw our neighbour farmer
waiting at the kerbside with his motor-bike. Much to my surprise,
he started to push his motorbike, and walk alongside us. Surprise is
not a strong enough word for what I felt when he asked me if I would
take a pillion lift home. I could only suppose that he didn't have the
nerve to ask Letty. She was so much prettier than I, and I then
judged feminine attraction simply by the face.

I was not enamoured of mine. 'More like a Chink's dial!' I used to
scold my reflection – high cheekbones, squat nose, wide mouth. That
I had grown to five feet six inches tall, with a tiny waist, and lovely
feminine proportions had quite escaped my notice. If I sound
immodest, it's because I saw, many years later, some snapshots
taken at the time. And if a modern sixteen-year-old miss thinks I
was ludicrously retarded, I was.

'Take Letty instead,' I offered haughtily, for I wanted none of his
charity.

'There isn't room for the two of you, and it's you I asked,' he said firmly, and quickly added, with some tact, 'Letty hasn't so far to go as you.'

'Go on, gal, have a ride,' urged Letty, I was so convinced of Letty's superiority, there was no need to feel pity for any slight, even unintended. Anyway, she had the two beaux behind her to choose from. I was also inwardly excited beyond measure at such a turn of events. So I couldn't resist accepting my moment of glory.

I took off my hat, and sat as gracefully as I could on the pillion. My heart was in my mouth, for more than one reason, when the motorbike chugged into life.

When we turned off the main road into the lane, the ride became very bumpy; but as soon as he got to the first gate on his land, he stopped and wheeled the bike inside. 'I'd like to walk you home the rest of the way,' he said.

At first he politely left a stranger's gap, bridged by mutual physical awareness between us; but suddenly, on pretext of an imaginary stumble, he took my arm. The pressure of his strong hand, firm yet gentle, pretending to hold me up, was very pleasing. But I was unpractised in coquetry, and it took nearly half a mile more before his arm got round my shoulder, with my head gently pressed against his chest.

The strong curve of a man's right arm is surely the dearest haven for a woman's head. By the time we had reached the horse-chestnut tree in the lane opposite Little Rowan, his arm had got down round my waist.

My instinctive woman's guile had been awakened during our walk, and I made a show of reluctance when he suggested we sit down under the chestnut tree. But slowly I allowed his tender male dominance to persuade me, and we were on the soft grass, he with his back against the trunk. Now I felt as helpless as a seedling that cannot resist the lure of the sun, forced by the very basis of its nature to grow, to bloom, and to seed.

I let the young man take me in his arms, tilt my unresisting face to his, gently brush my lips with his, searching for, and finding for both of us such a profound sweetness as I had never dreamed of. Everything beautiful I had ever known, or thought of, had lain dormant for this moment, to be awakened in this kiss. A kind of reverence came over us.

I could feel the pounding of my heart and his. It was just a kiss –

no more. But for me, new to the taste of love, it was enough, more than enough. The young man pulled me to my feet, and even the touching of our hands was ecstasy, and unabated till we reached the porch. Then, tenderly, as though I were made of gossamer, the young farmer kissed my lips, my forehead, and my work-roughened hands. 'I'll watch for you,' he whispered, and was gone.

It seemed as if I floated round to the back door. I wanted no supper. The cream pan did not tempt me to dip a finger. I could live without bread and drink tonight, for I had tasted nectar. I was sixteen and I had been kissed.

But Bert, poor Bert, still a clod-hopping mortal, he needed some supper. I was coming out of the dairy with the cheese for him when he clumped in through the door.

'I saw who brought you home tonight.' His voice sounded dour and accusing. 'When he realised I'd spotted him, he told me not to tell my uncle.'

He told him not tell his uncle! One minute I had been floating on the airy pinnacle of ecstasy, a Venus adored, and now I was the disowned beggarmaid, someone ashamed to have been seen with.

To have been escorted to the door of the Kingdom of Love, to have had my hand kissed like a queen, and then to have been snubbed so, and snubbed in front of someone like Bert!

At sixteen, black was black and white was white; it took years to merge them into grey. Lover to traitor, nectar to dust, I was still too full up for any supper. For now I was stuffed up with outraged feminine pride. By the time I got to bed it was overflowing from my eyes in two salty torrents.

Hitherto I had loved to waken in the morning to the pungent farmyard odours flavouring the new morning air, air that had come across the sea and over the top of the Sugar Loaf mountain. The soft feather bed did not compete too strongly with the new day beckoning through the window.

The waking sounds of birds and beasts, already heralded by the cock-crows near and far, gave importance to each day.

Come on, then, fowls! Fly from your perches, gobble up your scattered breakfast of golden corn.

Lumber ungainly up the lane, you cows, through the creaking, five-barred, wooden gate, into the rested field.

Don't wag your tail right off, old sheep dog, just because you are being let off your chain to manage, almost on your own, the moving of a hundred silly old sheep. Good dog, yes you are a good dog.

Stop your scolding quack-quack, you upstart ducks. I've got a lot of other jobs before I come to pull up the door of your pen.

Skinny sinuous cats, which of you were fighting like two Lucifers in the night? More ratting, and less tomming, you jealous Romeos. But here's your milk, all half a bucket of it, skimmed of course, to share between the six, seven, eight, oh, the lot of you.

There, I've seen to you all, but my heart's not in it any more; it's lying like lead in my side, and nobody knows, and nobody cares. I wish I was a cat, a sheep, a cow or a duck, you are somebody. I'm nobody, a proper nothing. No, I am a somebody; I'm Polly Mason, and I'll show him, oh, I'll show him! I'll walk by him, haughtier than any queen, if I ever set eyes on him again.

Set eyes on him again? Well, of all the cruel nerve! There he was, talking to the master by the granary door, and I must pass them to fetch some wood from the stack near the dog's kennel. I concentrated as much venom into the look I gave him as I then knew how to muster.

I threw the wood on the fire with enough angry carelessness to wake the baby, morning-napping in the wooden cradle on the floor. This brought me a sharp reprimand from the mistress to watch what I was doing.

I thought my master and mistress looked at me a bit quizzical when we were eating our dinner, but they made no comment on my behaviour.

It had not been the habit of the young farmer to call on my master, but now, to my annoyance and embarrassment, I could not help seeing them talking on several occasions. Once I was unlucky enough to answer the door to his knock. Luckily, the mistress was in the kitchen, for he held out his arms as though he would grab hold of me, and his eyes were as soft and begging as a spaniel's.

Let him do his underhand begging; I would not give him a bone if he were starving. I took great care to make myself scarce, and never to glance in his direction when he was about.

The village shop now delivered by van; I was half-glad, half-sorry that my weekly errand was finished. The exhilaration of feeling free for an hour or so was shadowed by the thought that I might bump into him.

It was a very cold autumn day when the shopkeeper forgot to bring our paraffin. We needed it for the lamps; I must put a move on with my chores and fetch it before dark.

On the way, I saw the cause of my misery walking behind a horse-drawn plough on his land some fields away. Away from the busy bustle of the farm, a deep sense of melancholy came over me. I would have to go away. I resolved to give in a month's notice the next day.

Hurrying home, changing the heavy can from one hand to the other to speed my progress, I was brought to a heart-pounding halt by the young farmer. He had been waiting behind the hedge near the last gate that bounded his land. He had stepped out in front of me and stood barring my way. Though already rosy-cheeked from exertion, I felt the blood rush to my face, and away from my legs.

I tried to side-step and pass him; I wanted none of his hole-in-the-corner attentions. With sheer strength he took the paraffin can from me, put an iron-hand grip on each of my shoulders, and backed me towards the gate. His manner was desperate and beseeching.

'Why do you keep hiding and turning away from me?' he begged, holding me in his arms against my will, and trying to find my lips with his.

Had I been a girl of true spirit I would have smacked his face and told him I was as good as he; and if he could not acknowledge openly he found me attractive, he could keep the secret all to himself.

Up till then my life had not done much to nurture such a spirit. I was full of inward pride, the sort that would cut off its nose to spite its face; the sort of pride that made a great fuss over the little it had to be proud about. I could not bear to put into words that hurt his slight had caused me. A week before, his kiss had made my body melt, yet now I felt as unyielding and unfeeling as the gate I was pressed against.

Puzzled and upset by my obstinacy, his ardour turned to anger; he let me go and walked back through the gate.

My mistress did not seem unduly upset when I gave her my month's notice. Though willing, I was not a particularly able servant. I found watching the floating myriads of dust particles highlighted in a shaft of sunlight through the window more amusing than polishing it off the furniture. Besides, I was getting a big girl with a big appetite; I was gone sixteen years old, and might be wanting a rise soon on my five-shilling-a-week wages. A livelier fourteen-year-old girl might be cheaper and easier to train.

I wrote home and told them I was leaving my job. Mam told a

neighbour, and the neighbour put this item of news in her letter to her daughter who was working in London. By this means, before I had left the farm I had a letter from my neighbour's daughter telling me she could get me a job any time. It would be working for Jewish people, as she was, and the wages were very good, ten shillings a week, and they did not mind if you did not wear caps and aprons. Her address was in Aldgate.

Supper was eaten in high good humour the evening before I left the farm. Bert and the master had taken all day to walk some bullocks into Abergavenny for sale, and they had fetched a very good price. Bert was as high and mighty as the Prince of Wales, with a new cap the guv'nor had bought him, and the master and mistress were oozing with good humour.

'We did wonder a while back,' smiled the master, winking at his wife, 'if we were going to have you for a neighbour in time. Poor Dai took a proper fancy to you, you know, neglecting his own place, finding excuses to come across to see me. I knew who he'd really come to see. Mind you, he asked me all above board if it would be all right for him to take you out. I could tell by the way you looked at him he wasn't going to have any luck. You could have done worse, you know. There's many a girl round here would jump at the chance of him.'

The piece of broth-soaked bread I had just spooned into my mouth waited there to be swallowed; to go down with the surprise, the shame, the remorse and helplessness I felt trying to cope with the multiplicity of emotions these remarks had waked.

What an upstart! What an intolerant misjudger of character! What a fool I had been!

I like to think that if I had been a free agent, I would have jumped up from the table and run to make some apology. It is self-delusion. I had not the grace of character, the wit, or the experience to handle the situation. I had burned my boats, and I had fallen out of love. All the same I took remorse to bed with me that night, and it allowed me very little sleep.

(from *A Child in the Forest*)

The Interview

Imagine that Winifred Foley is being interviewed about this passage from her book. Choose some of the following questions to put to her and write your answers as though you were the author herself.

1. Did it never occur to you that Bert might have been lying when he said the young farmer asked him not tell his uncle?
2. You seemed a bit surprised that the young farmer should want to see you home rather than Letty. Why were you unaware that you were attractive?
3. Wouldn't it have been better to have had it out with him when he visited the farm or when he waylaid you in the lane? Why couldn't you speak to him about it?
4. What do you think he was thinking about you when you ignored him? After all, he didn't know what Bert had told you, did he?
5. Running through the episode is a note of regret – as though you are accusing yourself for not behaving differently. Were you to be blamed? Was it all your fault?
6. Can you express what you felt when the master told you the truth that evening?
7. To return to your self-criticism. You say that you were 'haughty', that your face was like 'a Chink's dial', that you were full of pride, that you were an upstart, a fool! You don't let yourself off lightly, do you? But there was obviously another side to your nature and your appearance. What would you say this was?
8. Would you have been a good farmer's wife, do you think?

Class Conversation

In this extract Polly buys some new clothes *to impress the boys back home*. Have you bought any new clothes recently? What was at the back of your mind when you bought them? How do you feel when you wear them?

The two boys following Polly and Letty after chapel were making their first steps in getting acquainted with the girls. 'Following' was a popular way of getting to know girls in those days. How do teenagers get to know one another now?

Polly's pride was hurt by the suggestion that she was socially inferior to the farmer. Are you aware of social differences in your own life? On what are the differences based? How do they affect your attitude towards other people?

The sudden change from love to hate, from wonderful happiness to great despondency: have you ever experienced any similar fluctuation of mood? What can put you into a state of happiness or gloom and what can bring you out of it?

Polly found immense satisfaction in the sounds of the farmyard and in the characters of the farm animals. What have you found interesting in the individual characters of birds and animals? Can you give some examples?

Word-study

Write out the following quotations from the passage and after each one give a brief explanation of the word in bold type:

page 124: *a **frugal** but healthy diet* (line 3)
*in such a **transport** of good humour* (line 25)
page 125: *who did all the **chores*** (line 1)
*I walked proud and **sedate*** (line 19)
*considering the **sparseness** of the local population* (line 36)
page 126: *the description savoured of **swank*** (line 1)
*to escape **surveillance** of our elders* (line 10)
***gauche** and unsure like dog puppies* (line 13)
*bold and **diffident** by turns* (line 13)
*I was not **enamoured** of mine* (line 32)
*high cheekbones, **squat** nose, wide mouth* (line 33)
*I was **ludicrously** retarded* (line 37)
page 127: *there was no need to feel pity for any **slight,** even unintended* (line 5)
*she had the two **beaux** behind her to choose from* (line 6)
*on **pretext** of an imaginary stumble* (line 17)
*I was unpractised in **coquetry*** (line 19)
*my instinctive woman's **guile*** (line 27)
page 128: *the touching of our hands was ecstasy, and **unabated*** (line 2)

> *as though I was made of* **gossamer** (line 4)
> *for I had tasted* **nectar** (line 9)
> *his voice sounded* **dour** *and accusing* (line 14)
> *the* **pungent** *farmyard odours* (line 28)
> *lumber* **ungainly** *up the lane* (line 37)

page 129: *skinny* **sinuous** *cats* (line 4)
I concentrated as much **venom** *into the look I gave him* (line 16)
my master and mistress looked at me a bit **quizzical** (line 23)

page 130: *his* **ardour** *turned to anger* (line 30)
the floating **myriads** *of dust particles* (line 34)

Your own writing

1. Marriages cannot take place unless one of the partners makes a proposal and the other accepts it. It must be happening every day of the week, in all kinds of places. Some of these proposals are 'romantic', others are down-to-earth and practical. Write a sketch or a short story depicting your idea of a modern proposal of marriage.

2. What emotional problems occur amongst teenagers today? Give one or two examples of relationships that began well but ended unhappily. What, or who, was to blame?

3. Buying and wearing new clothes:
   a) a story centering on the arguments that arise at home when you buy the 'wrong' thing;
   b) describe some of the latest fashions in the form of an article for a newspaper or magazine;
   c) a short play or story in which a sales assistant tries to sell a customer a particular article of clothing.

4. Describe the events in the passage from the point of view of Dai, the young farmer who fell in love with Polly.

5. Develop a piece of writing of your own based on one of these quotations from the passage:
   a) 'Don't turn round, but, indeed, they are following us.'
   b) 'Surprise is not a strong enough word for what I felt when he asked me if I would take a pillion lift home.'

c) *'The soft feather bed did not compete too strongly with the new day beckoning through the window.'*

d) *'What a fool I had been!'*

6. Write on one or more of the topics discussed in 'Class Conversation'.

Honda 175
Eddie Wainwright

Dry-eyed, fist in a sling, his glossy hobby-horse
Battle-scarred and blooded in its first
Encounter with a stony world: I grieved for this,

Remembering all his pride as he roared off,
Reckless and unassailable; grieve for his generation
Which shrugs away pain I more resent.

I have no love for the machine, but would have wept
And cursed had I been him. These neo-Stoics
Frighten me. Their joys and hates dispose

As easily as tissue. What became of the boy
Who saw his kitten laid out on a spade
Ready for burial after the butcher's van

Had bundled it like offal to the gutter?
You gazed at it in stricken disbelief,
Gathered your strength upstairs, and shaped a grave,

And wrapped her in a decent rag. White mice
Devoured by marauding cats in the garden shed:
It isn't fair, you cried: it wasn't. Nor was this.

Perhaps each fresh assault should numb the soul
A little more, perhaps it is unnatural

To mourn his blackened hand and buckled wheel.

Living without illusions, he will never
Bruise to the core, and bikes can be repaired.
I ransack drawers for his insurance papers.

Considering the poem

1. What details of the accident are given in the poem?
2. Stoics were ancient Greek philosophers who practised rigorous self-denial and were indifferent to pleasure and pain. Why does Eddie Wainwright refer to his son and others like him as *these neo-Stoics*?
3. Which sentence in the poem implies that the poet does not consider himself to be a Stoic?
4. Can you explain what point Eddie Wainwright is making in introducing the references to the dead kitten and the white mice that were devoured by cats?
5. Do you think the son was really as unconcerned about the accident as his father suggests?

Class Conversation

What puzzled the father most about his son's attitude towards the accident?

Would you say it was typical of your generation to be indifferent to the pain and suffering caused by accidents on motorbikes? Does this apply to all sport?

Have you any experience of accidents? What happened? How did people react?

What disagreements have you known to be caused in families over the buying of bicycles, motorbikes, scooters, skateboards or cars? What points of view are expressed – and who usually wins?

What are the laws about the ownership and driving of motorised vehicles? Are these laws enforced and observed?

Have you any desire to own a vehicle?

Your own writing

1. Write a short play or a dialogue for two or three characters on: a family argument about buying a motorbike or scooter; *or* the excitements, pleasures and risks of riding motorbikes.
2. Imagine that you have been asked to write a short handbook for young people about owning their first motorbike – or any other type of vehicle. Under suitable headings – such as Buying, Maintenance, What the Law Says, Clubs, etc – give some useful information and advice to the prospective owners of new vehicles.
3. Write a poem or an essay on the pleasure you have had from owning a vehicle of any kind.
4. Many people react with horror to the intentional or accidental killing of animals. Write about a personal experience of the death of an animal or bird; or express your opinion of the killing of wildlife for sport or commercial gain.
5. On what subjects do the generations differ? Give some examples in the form of an essay, a story or a play of the contrasting and conflicting attitudes of different generations towards life today.

How to Grow Old
Bertrand Russell

During his long life Bertrand Russell was a mathematician, a philosopher, an educationist, a writer and, in his later years, a vigorous campaigner for world peace and nuclear disarmament. He was born in 1872 and died in 1970. He was, therefore, well qualified to write this essay.

In spite of the title, this article will really be on how not to grow old, which, at my time of life, is a much more important subject. My first advice would be to choose your ancestors carefully. Although both my parents died young, I have done well in this respect as regards my other ancestors. My maternal grandfather, it is true, was cut off in the flower of his youth at the age of sixty-seven, but my other three grandparents all lived to be over eighty. Of remoter ancestors I can only discover one who did not live to a great age, and he died of a disease which is now rare, namely, having his head cut off. A great-grandmother of mine, who was a friend of Gibbon, lived to the age of ninety-two, and to her last day remained a terror to all her descendants. My maternal grandmother, after having nine children who survived, one who died in infancy, and many miscarriages, as soon as she became a widow devoted herself to women's higher education. She was one of the founders of Girton College, and worked hard at opening the medical profession to women. She used to relate how she met in Italy an elderly gentleman who was looking very sad. She inquired the cause of his melancholy and he said he had just departed from his two grandchildren. 'Good gracious,' she exclaimed, 'I have seventy-two grandchildren, and if I were sad each time I parted from one of them, I should have a dismal existence!' 'Madre snaturale,' he replied. (Unnatural mother). But speaking as one of the seventy-two, I prefer her recipe. After the age of eighty she found she had some difficulty in getting to sleep, so she habitually spent the hours from midnight to 3 a.m. in reading popular science. I do not believe that she ever had time to notice that she was growing old. This, I think, is the proper recipe for remaining young. If you have wide and keen interests and activities in which you can still be effective, you will have no reason to think about the merely statistical fact of the number of years you have already lived, still less the probable brevity of your future.

As regards health, I have nothing useful to say, since I have little experience of illness. I eat and drink whatever I like, and sleep when I cannot keep awake. I never do anything whatever on the ground that it is good for health, though in actual fact the things I like doing are mostly wholesome.

Psychologically there are two dangers to be guarded against in old age. One of these is undue absorption in the past. It does not do to live in memories, in regrets for the good old days, or in sadness about friends who are dead. One's thoughts must be directed to the future, and to things about which there is something to be done. This is not always easy; one's own past is a gradually increasing weight. It is easy to think to oneself that one's emotions used to be more vivid than they are, and one's mind more keen. If this is true it should be forgotten, and if it is forgotten it will probably not be true.

The other thing to be avoided is clinging to youth in the hope of sucking vigour from its vitality. When your children are grown up they want to live their own lives, and if you continue to be as interested in them as you were when they were young, you are likely to become a burden to them, unless they are unusually callous. I do not mean that one should be without interest in them, but one's interest should be contemplative and, if possible, philanthropic, but not unduly emotional. Animals become indifferent to their young as soon as their young can look after themselves, but human beings, owing to the length of infancy, find this difficult.

I think that a successful old age is easiest for those who have strong impersonal interests involving appropriate activities. It is in this sphere that long experience is really fruitful, and it is in this sphere that the wisdom born of experience can be exercised without being oppressive. It is no use telling grown-up children not to make mistakes, both because they will not believe you, and because mistakes are an essential part of education. But if you are one of those who are incapable of impersonal interests, you may find that your life will be empty unless you concern yourself with your children and grandchildren. In that case you must realise that while you can still render them material services, such as making them an allowance or knitting them jumpers, you must not expect that they will enjoy your company.

Some old people are oppressed by the fear of death. In the young there is a justification for this feeling. Young men who have reason to fear that they will be killed in battle may justifiably feel bitter in the thought that they have been cheated of the best things that life has to offer. But in an old man who has known human joys and sorrows, and has achieved whatever work it was in him to do, the fear of death is somewhat abject and ignoble. The best way to overcome it – so at least it seems to me – is to make your interests gradually wider and more impersonal, until bit by bit the walls of the ego recede, and your life becomes increasingly merged in the universal life. An individual human existence should be like a river – small at first, narrowly contained within its banks, and rushing passionately past boulders and over waterfalls. Gradually the river grows wider, the banks recede, the waters flow more quietly, and in the end, without any visible break, they become merged in the sea, and painlessly lose their individual being. The man who, in old age, can see his life in this way, will not suffer from the fear of death, since the things he cares for will continue. And if, with the decay of vitality, weariness increases, the thought of rest will be not unwelcome. I should wish to die while still at work, knowing that others will carry on what I can no longer do, and content in the thought that what was possible has been done.

The Interview

Write your answers to the questions as though you were the author himself.

1. Most of your ancestors lived to a ripe old age and, as you say, you chose them well! Does it follow that the reverse is also true – that if your ancestors died young you are likely to die young also?

2. Since I am likely to be an ancestor myself at some time in the future, how should I go about being a *good* ancestor?
3. Speaking of the old person's attitude towards his grown-up children you say, *if you continue to be as interested in them as you were when they were young, you are likely to be a burden to them,* **unless they are unusually callous.** Could you explain a little more what you mean by this last phrase?
4. What would a *contemplative* and a *philanthropic* attitude be?
5. What do you see wrong with an *emotional* attitude?
6. You make the distinction between personal and impersonal interests. Can you give us one or two examples of what you mean by 'impersonal interests'?
7. In the river of life metaphor, what actual periods of life – and what activities associated with them – are you thinking of when you speak of, first, the river's being *narrowly contained within its banks* and, secondly, *rushing passionately past boulders and over waterfalls*?
8. You write from the experience of a successful old age. How much was due to good luck and how much to what one might call good management?

Class Conversation

How far back can you trace your ancestors? What interesting facts do you know about them?

In your own family is the company of grandparents enjoyed or not, both by your parents and by yourself? In other words, is Bertrand Russell right or wrong?

Russell's is a philosopher's view of old age. Does it avoid the realities? What aspects of old age are not touched on in the essay?

Russell says he would like to die while still at work. Do you know any old people who are still working or occupying themselves in useful pursuits?

What problems are created by old age? How are they usually dealt with?

Language

1. The word *maternal* comes from the Latin word for *mother,* which is *mater.* Can you find some more English words – and their meanings – which derive from these other members of the Latin family? *pater* (father), *frater* (brother), *soror* (sister), *filius* (son), *avunculus* (uncle), *uxor* (wife).
2. A *philanthropist* is defined in the Concise Oxford Dictionary as 'a lover of mankind; one who exerts himself for the well-being of his fellow men'. Can you find the meaning of these related words, which contain either *phil* (lover of) or *anthropos* (man)? *misanthropist Anglophil philhellene anthropologist anthropoid.*
3. What is the meaning in the essay of *a)* abject and *b)* ignoble?
4. Write definitions of these three related psychological terms: ego id libido.
5. The essay is divided into six clearly defined paragraphs. The first deals with Bertrand Russell's *family ancestors;* the second with *health.* Can you give a similar short phrase to describe the subject of each of the remaining paragraphs?

Your own writing

1. Write an essay on the subject: How to be young. Take some ideas from the structure of Bertrand Russell's essay. For instance, you could consider paragraphs on: the importance of parents; how to remain healthy in body and mind; the 'dangers' that beset modern youth and how to tackle them; how to enjoy yourself; how to prepare for a successful maturity.
2. My ancestors. You could do some family research and write factually about a few of your ancestors, devoting a paragraph to each one (though you should not spill the family beans, nor reveal skeletons in cupboards!). Alternatively, you could create an entirely fictitious set of ancestors and endow them with some entertaining eccentricities.
3. Many people nowadays go to great lengths to promote their own health. Choose one or two typical examples and write either a conversation between two health addicts or a single speech in which a person talks about his or her techniques for remaining healthy. An alternative is simply to devote separate paragraphs to various modern ways of achieving health.

4. Describe some of the ways in which old people are helped in our society. Can you suggest any improvements?
5. A letter to a grandparent.
6. 'Mistakes are an essential part of education.'
7. Write on one or more of the topics discussed during 'Class Conversation'.

Poem for my Father
Graham Allen

Old fellow, old one,
sing me a song out of the dark,
a scullery one, and I'll beat time still
on the tin bath.
How clear you looked free of the work's dirt
and gay with evening, your time for taking the air
– you'd think breathing it was a work of art,
my mother said.
Sometimes before dressing, suds long at the elbow,
you had me punch away at your bicep:
always this strength; always the body,
you tested everything on it,
all life's fifty-year long shift:
suddenly, you must lie down with its strange stillness.

Older, I thought all you left of yourself
at home was a black ring round that bath,
water down the drain,
and me, cold leavings,
to remind my mother bitterly of you.
But do you remember sometimes on nights,
out of the street's noise never got used to,
you slept in my back-room, slipped carefully
into the rumpled shape of warmth I left you there,
each morning that ghostly crossing, you worn-out,
me head-full of Donne, Shakespeare and Keats?

– *Hyperion* to you was a beery windfall.
Now I get you into bed and out of it,
ashamed.
My body was never my meal-ticket
in the burrow of street and foundry under
the rattling viaduct, the canal's dark bridges.
Do you think if I could give you this strength
I wouldn't?
With finger-tip touch I steady your shoulders
pretending you sit alone on the brand-new commode.

Old fellow, old one,
sing me a song out of the dark,
twenty years later,
(must it be twenty years late?)
let the morning find
that shared shape in the bed,
– no more cold crossings for us –
but the same flesh and warmth and need,
a father, a son.

Considering the poem

1. The theme of the poem is the changing relationship between the writer and his father. What incidents in Graham Allen's early childhood show that at first the relationship was a happy one?
2. Which lines indicate that as the boy grew up there was a rift between himself and his father?
3. Father's coming in from the night shift and the son's going out in the morning to school is described as *that ghostly crossing*. What made each character seem 'ghostly'?
4. *Hyperion* is the title of a poem by Keats, but it was also the name of a famous race horse. What do you think a *beery windfall* would be?
5. What are the chief differences between father and son?
6. The poem ends by suggesting the essential closeness of the relationship between father and son. What has brought about this closeness?

7. What detail in the poem symbolises this closeness or unity?
8. What difficulties have you found in understanding this poem? Is there anything that still remains unclear to you?

Your own writing

You will see that the poem is written in a very 'free' style, without regular verses, with varying line-lengths and with an absence of rhyme. It is very much like the poet writing down thoughts and memories as they came to him. Write a 'free verse' poem of your own, using one of the following suggestions:

1. Changed relationships as you have grown older: with childhood friends, with parents, with other members of your family.
2. A relationship with a person who has become ill.
3. The street's noises.
4. Family comings and goings.
5. The thoughts and feelings of a worker 'on nights'.